Also by Deborah Owens

NICKEL AND DIME YOUR WAY TO WEALTH

CONFIDENT INVESTING: A WEALTH-BUILDING GUIDE FOR WOMEN

EVERYWOMAN'S MONEY: CONFIDENT INVESTING

A PURSE OF YOUR OWN

AN EASY GUIDE TO FINANCIAL SECURITY

DEBORAH OWENS

WITH BRENDA LANE RICHARDSON

A Fireside Book
Published by Simon & Schuster
New York   London   Toronto   Sydney

This publication contains the opinions and ideas of its author. It is sold with the understanding that neither the author nor the publisher is engaged in rendering legal, tax, investment, insurance, financial, accounting, or other professional advice or services. If the reader requires such advice or services, a competent professional should be consulted. The strategies outlined in this book may not be suitable for every individual, and are not guaranteed or warranted to produce any particular results.

No warranty is made with respect to the accuracy or completeness of the information contained in this book (including for the content of any third party website referenced herein), and both the author and the publisher specifically disclaim any responsibility for any liability, loss or risk, personal or otherwise, which is incurred as a consequence, directly or indirectly, of the use and application of any of the contents of this book.

Fireside
A Division of Simon & Schuster, Inc.
1230 Avenue of the Americas
New York, NY 10020

Copyright © 2010 by Deborah Owens and Brenda Richardson

All rights reserved, including the right to reproduce this book or portions thereof in any form whatsoever. For information address Fireside Subsidiary Rights Department, 1230 Avenue of the Americas, New York, NY 10020.

First Fireside paperback edition January 2010

Fireside and colophon are registered trademarks of Simon & Schuster, Inc.

For information about special discounts for bulk purchases, please contact Simon & Schuster Special Sales at 1-866-506-1949 or business@simonandschuster.com

The Simon & Schuster Speakers Bureau can bring authors to your live event. For more information or to book an event, contact the Simon & Schuster Speakers Bureau at 1-866-248-3049 or visit our website at www.simonspeakers.com.

Designed by Lisa Stokes

Manufactured in the United States of America

10 9 8 7 6 5 4 3 2

Library of Congress Cataloging-in-Publication Data
Owens, Deborah.
    A purse of your own : an easy guide to financial security / Deborah Owens, with Brenda Lane Richardson.
        p.   cm.
"A Fireside Book."
    1. Women—Finance, Personal.   2. Investments.   3. Finance, Personal.   I. Richardson, Brenda Lane.   II. Title.
    HG179.O868 2010
    332.024'01082—dc22   2009035662

ISBN 978-1-4165-7081-3
ISBN 978-1-4165-7108-7 (eBook)

Deborah Owens:

This book is dedicated to my mother, Erma Thomas, who is the inspiration for my life's work and whose own purse is filled with love and generosity.

Brenda Lane Richardson:

This book is dedicated to Dr. W. Mark Richardson, my husband and BFF.

CONTENTS

USING YOUR PURSE FOR PROTECTION

THE INCIDENT IS SAID TO HAVE OCCURRED ON A rain-soaked road near Dallas. Four older women were riding in an Impala when a vehicle sped through a red light and smashed into them, the impact sending their car spinning. Although clearly at fault, the other driver, a male, climbed out and approached with his hands thrown up, as if to say that *he'd had it* with women drivers. If this man hoped to intimidate these "little old ladies," his plan backfired.

The Impala's driver rolled down her window and when the man said something that made her feel threatened, she blasted him with pepper spray and jabbed him with an umbrella. According to an eyewitness, the women then climbed from their car and hit him with their purses until he fled for safety.

Admittedly, I have a different kind of protection in mind when I travel the country to speak about the power of the purse or talk to listeners who call into *Wealthy Lifestyles,* my financial show on WEAA 88.9 FM, an NPR-affiliate station in Baltimore. But the idea of women banding together to become active participants in their own lives—in this case, clobbering a bully with their purses—offers an indelible image for a concept that I teach about how the purse can provide protection.

The power of the purse message has been especially welcome since 2008, when the world economy has seemed in free fall and millions have panicked as they watched their nest eggs and retirement funds shrink dramatically. These are the times when novices want to know how to hang on to their purses.

The financial meltdown that began in 2007 was caused by people leading what I call "unwealthy lifestyles." Too much house furnished with multiple mortgage refinancing, and too much credit card use with ever-increasing interest rate terms. Those same exotic mortgages were then packaged into investment securities that Wall Street sold all over the world, which eventually turned into toxic waste on the balance sheets of icons in the financial industry such as American Insurance Group (AIG) and Merrill Lynch. The real estate bubble bursting impacted the financial system in ways no one could have imagined, and at this writing caused the stock market to lose more than half its worth in less than twelve months. As a result, people have become more averse to investing. But as the dust clears, you can be sure that new fortunes will be made. And why shouldn't yours be one of them? Investing remains the best long-term vehicle for acquiring wealth.

Women in my audiences may be fainthearted, but they are comforted by the symbol of the purse, an accessory that is near and dear. They seem to get my message right away when I say that the financial sector became lopsided, with way too much debt and too little real wealth, like a purse weighed down by thousands of pennies. *Purse* is all about restoring equilibrium and creating financially and emotionally balanced investors.

I use the purse as a metaphor for wealth because it dates back to antiquity when it represented a woman's dowry, her family's way of making certain that she was entering a relationship with recognized assets. Today, when so many of us call the shots about our own lives, the purse speaks to our financial state of mind. A full purse can provide opportunities for leaving a bruising relationship; an empty one may mean having to stay and suffer more.

The purse has long been a reflection of our economic power. When husbands controlled the assets of Victorian women, the purse was dainty, designed for carrying calling cards and hankies. During World War II, as women took over nontraditional "Rosie the Riveter" jobs, sturdier purses became fashionable. At war's end, when soldiers returned to the States and the workplace, women were again relegated to the home and purses dwindled in size.

Now, as if mirroring our move into the highest corridors of power, purses are built to accommodate everything from wallets, checkbooks, calculators, cell phones, and corporate reports to lipstick, earrings, tissues, and baby's emergency diaper and wipes. Today's purses seem to represent all the possibilities in our lives.

Whether you carry a designer knockoff or a high-priced object of impulse and lust, a purse is probably your most intimate accessory. If you can't locate it, your heart races; alone on a dark street, you clutch it beneath an arm. And no matter how much you love someone, if that person rifles through our purse, you feel violated. There is deep sympathetic meaning to be found in our purses. More than a simple repository for objects, they are extensions of who we are. Freud interpreted the purse as female genitalia, but that was a nineteenth-century man's explanation. More than anything, the purse represents our private financial identity. At the end of the day, creating wealth is about adding to the purse.

For the most part, purses have remained quintessentially female. One manufacturer tried popularizing the use of "man bags" for guys, but the idea never really caught on. In the United States, in particular, men largely view purses as girly girl, and that's all right with me. I like the idea of having a financial identity that is distinctly female, like this investment guide. *A Purse of Your Own* accentuates investment strategies for building wealth based on our unique mélange of strengths, whatever that means for you as an individual. This work capitalizes on interests that include friendships, parenting, romance, dieting, and shopping.

Do those subjects sound familiar? That's right, ladies, I'm throwing down the gauntlet and embracing what's nearest and dearest to our hearts. From this point on, the purse stops here. I'm sick of hearing that we've got to act like one of the guys to get ahead financially. That certainly hasn't been the case for two of the richest women on the planet, J. K. Rowling, of *Harry Potter* fame and entertainment powerhouse Oprah Winfrey. And you've got to wonder what Winfrey and Rowling know that others don't.

Rowling was distraught after her marriage ended. She might have been written off as "too emotional" and too "clingy," except she used her understanding of the universal need to feel loved to write Harry Potter into the world history of literature. Winfrey, among the first to insist that friendships between women matter, built an entertainment empire by using the alchemy of her body, mind, and spirit to make us feel that's she's right there with us when we need her guidance, laughter, knowledge, and inspiration—as a BFF should be.

It's as if Rowling and Winfrey were listening to Nelson Mandela's

1994 inauguration speech when he reminded the world that humans are powerful beyond measure and that it is our light, not our darkness, that frightens us. Rowling and Winfrey understand that the feminine spirit illuminates the world. These women are not afraid to let their lights shine.

Rowling and Winfrey exemplify generosity, creativity, and a desire for relationships—all of which are considered "feminine" characteristics. At the same time, they're also ambitious, analytical, and fearless, traits many considered "masculine." By drawing from these characteristics, each woman has created a purse that runneth over.

Just as there are two sides to every purse, there are two sides to every personality: female and male. That is not a new concept. Psychotherapist Carl Jung posited decades ago that both men and women are born with the psychological attitudes and feelings of the opposite sex and that a harmonious balance can only be established by expressing hidden traits. He was suggesting that we all embody a full spectrum of masculine and feminine qualities.

What is new is that *Purse* encourages the utilization of female/male energy to learn and practice balanced investment techniques. Consider the investors who've made headlines in recent years by contributing to a global financial malaise. The only kind of balance they focused on was the numeric value of their bank accounts. *Purse* stresses the importance of maintaining an emotional balance. Expressing one side of the personality to the exclusion of the other can leave people feeling disconnected from themselves.

All human beings are unique, of course. Our personalities are influenced by the interplay of hormones, genetic inheritance, family experiences, and societal expectations about female/male roles. Feminine energy isn't limited to women, nor is male energy limited to men. In more than two decades as an investment specialist, I've run into many people who seem out of balance. The women are often reluctant to tap into masculine strengths that would allow them to take risks and go for their dreams. They often wind up desperately searching for men who can fulfill their dreams for them. I've also met male investors who took risks purely for risk's sake, without any apparent thought about who might get hurt. Their absence of compassion and their inability to connect with others ultimately cost them everything, including their money and loved ones.

My purse strategy is designed to help people feel more balanced even in the middle of a financial storm. Feminine attributes can serve as a counterbalance to masculine attributes, and vice versa. Admirable female strengths include being adaptable, humble, empathic, compassionate, persuasive, spontaneous, receptive, nurturing, intuitive, verbal, and sensitive. Admirable masculine characteristics include being ambitious, assertive, confident, disciplined, courageous, decisive, organized, analytical, competitive, independent, and rational. Please note that while I believe that women and men possess all these strengths, I refer to them with "male" or "female" designations for the purpose of calling attention to propensities, not as rigid determinations of gender.

A Purse of Your Own taps into female/male energy and offers a practical application to investment basics. Tapping into feminine/masculine strengths has already helped men and women create fortunes. Mary Kay Ash, founder of Mary Kay Cosmetics, and Fred Smith, founder of Federal Express, both credit their success in part to knowing how to balance intuition with rational data. And the female genius of forming and nurturing relationships is increasingly touted in business schools. Dartmouth University Tuck School of Business Professor Vijay Govindarajan teaches future leaders that along with intellectual and physical infrastructures, successful companies also need emotional infrastructure.

I became interested in how people can strike a financial balance more than two decades ago, when life gave me an image of what I didn't want my future to be like. Years earlier, my mother quit her job at the Chrysler auto plant in Detroit and moved to Hawaii with my father, who had long dreamed of living on the island. But the two later separated, and my mother had to survive on a small pension, Social Security, and minimal support from my father.

With family money tight, I dropped out of college to manage a women's clothing store in Detroit, sometimes working sixteen hours a day. Though twenty years old, I realized that even by working excessively, I wouldn't have enough hours in the day to create wealth. I was earning enough to pay bills, but it was obvious that if I kept going at this rate, I'd be carrying a "Counterfeit Purse"—that's my term for the symbolic bag that some of us may carry, who might dress fashionably and drive a nice car but have nothing of real value. Like counterfeit purses sold on the streets, these bags might look great at first glance, but they won't hold up to wear.

At some point I heard from a friend who'd been hired by Merrill Lynch, the financial management and advisory firm. She explained that wealthy people invested their money so it would work for them, rather than the other way around. I was thrilled at the idea that I could invest money in a business or government enterprise, with an eye on earning future potential profit. I didn't realize it at the time, but this was when I began developing an understanding of the world that I would formalize into a defining set of behaviors, ultimately calling them the 7 Wealthy Habits. The first pertains to what I had searched for and then realized through investing: the ability to add value.

A WEALTHY OUTLOOK: This foundational habit gives us a macro or "big picture" view of the world. It is a habit that encourages adding value. It is characteristic of successful people and a core value of great companies, allowing them to move beyond boundaries.

I applied at Merrill Lynch and when I learned that the only job available was as a receptionist, I jumped at it so I could get my foot in the door. I loved talking to people and I was intrigued by the business of investing. In my spare time I read *The Wall Street Journal* so I could learn the language of finance and speak intelligently about what was happening in the industry. I couldn't get enough information—another wealth-building behavior. This hunger to learn taught me another Wealthy Habit.

A WEALTHY APPETITE: The habit of acquiring knowledge. To add value, wealthy people continually increase their knowledge base. They gain insight by attending seminars, subscribing to periodicals, and reading books to stay abreast of the economy and to identify investment opportunities.

I'd been hired in what some people in the office viewed as a rather low-level job, but I didn't let the job define me. The branch manager told me eventually that I was overqualified. I was encouraged to take the Series 7 securities certification exam to qualify to train as a

registered sales assistant. This experience exemplifies another wealth-building behavior.

A WEALTHY VISION: Rather than the macro view required in the first habit, a Wealthy Vision encourages you to look inward and identify your comparative advantage—your unique gifts based upon a blend of innate characteristics.

I heard horror stories from co-workers about how difficult it was to pass the Series 7 exam. Some said it would take several tries before I could pass. That filled me with dread. Guys who had been hired as assistant brokers were allowed to study and take prep classes on company time. No such luck for me. My purse was running on empty. I was supporting myself on my receptionist salary. I studied when I got home, and all through the weekends. I couldn't afford to fail—and I didn't. I passed the exam on the first try, and was promoted to a registered sales assistant with a higher salary.

A WEALTHY MINDSET: This habit keeps you going in the face of adversity. Everyone else might tell you something is impossible, but a Wealthy Mindset keeps you moving to the beat of your own drum.

I was hired to train under and work for three male brokers, but the broker I most admired was a woman named Emmo. She was the first woman I'd met who earned six figures. More important, she represented a wonderful balance of female/male energy. She was assertive, analytical, fearless, creative, nurturing, and generous. Emmo was a phenomenal presenter and led seminars in schools and for many women's groups. She would speak anywhere about her passion for investing, even when she might have stayed in the office and earned money. She also modeled another wealthy behavior for me.

A WEALTHY LEGACY: Promotes the importance of paying your way forward. To receive, you must first give something of value. People who develop this habit recognize that it is in giving that they receive, and they relish the opportunity to leave a path for others to follow. They understand the need for estate planning and charitable giving.

I was learning a lot in my day job as a registered sales assistant, but I volunteered to work for Emmo in the evening without pay, if she would become my mentor. Emmo refused to let me work for free. She said she hated doing a lot of the paperwork associated with her job and calling clients to confirm purchases. If I handled those for her, she said, she'd pay me 10 percent of her commissions, which far outstripped my salary. Of course I accepted, and became her most ardent employee, keeping her organized and on track, and I became her acolyte—learning not only the nuances of investing, but also how to speak so people would listen. My new income filled my purse. I started saving money, and as soon as I had a comfortable nest egg, I started making investments of my own. Setting up a system of support to build wealth is an outgrowing of another key behavior.

A WEALTHY SYSTEM: Successful people set up a system that allows them to remain organized. This is the habit that allows them to track resources, manage their finances, and adopt money management and investment processes that allow them to monitor their progress.

Determined to succeed, in 1986 I accepted an offer from Fidelity Investments to work as a financial consultant. I had been dating my now-husband Terry for a few years and he had recently gotten hired as a television news producer at the local affiliate in Detroit. We married and although I gave birth to our son, Brandon, a year later, my career at Fidelity moved on an upward trajectory. My hard work and efforts were starting to pay off. Fidelity tapped me to become a management trainee and after training for eight weeks in Boston, I was assigned to become an assistant manager in San Francisco. My husband quit his job as a news producer and we arrived in San Francisco in 1989. I continued to progress through the ranks at Fidelity and two years later, I was named regional sales manager of the West Coast. I had reached my first major goal, which brings me to a last and equally important wealthy behavior.

A WEALTHY FOCUS: This habit helps you remain determined, set priorities, and eliminate distractions as you pursue goals. Wealthy people recognize that stating specific desired outcomes allows them to stay on course even when dealing with complications.

I used these seven Wealthy Habits in concert. They lifted blinders from my eyes, helping me to see what others could not, and then gave me the confidence to take risks that I might otherwise have avoided. One of the biggest risks involved me investing in my own dreams. I loved my new job and the privileges it conferred. But beating beneath the breast pocket of my Ann Taylor suits was the heart of a rebel. I've always enjoyed the idea of sticking a lacquered fingernail in the eye of conventional wisdom, especially when it comes to teaching women personal finance.

....

As I watched male colleagues try to convince women to adopt a hyperaggressive, win-at-any-cost attitude toward investing, I saw many an eye glaze over. It was obvious that it was the *approaches* that weren't catching on, not the women. What made me certain? Well, think of what life is like for us. We're often the ones who find what everybody else is looking for—the missing sock, book, mayonnaise at the back of the refrigerator, or Donna Karan in the pile of irregulars. Investing is made for our kind of thinking. Our brains are wired for doing many things at once. Investing is fast, moves quickly; it takes some planning and flexibility. We can fit it into busy lives; prepare it

now and pick it up later. It's interesting and makes for good conversation, if only we would start talking about it. But for the most part, that conversation was mainly happening among guys.

I saw this situation and wanted to do something to address it. The question was whether I'd have the courage to give up a high-salaried position. As my career flourished, my husband freelanced as a television reporter in San Francisco and Los Angeles. He eventually accepted a position as a news reporter at the ABC affiliate in Baltimore and we relocated immediately afterward. I also gave birth to our daughter, Olivia, in 1992. Fidelity was extremely supportive and transferred me to a position as branch manager vice president in Washington, DC. After several years of live-in nannies and child care disasters, I told Terry that I longed to venture out on my own, to introduce the world of investing to groups that were underrepresented in the field, particularly women. He encouraged me to go for it.

....

In 1996, in addition to launching a career as a financial radio host, I founded Owens Media Group LLC to develop seminars and workshops for nonprofit organizations. The goal of the radio show, *Real Money,* was to encourage people of all incomes to build wealth. My new show *Wealthy Lifestyles* airs weekly on the NPR affiliate in Baltimore, and as of this writing, we are gearing up for national syndication. The show has given me an opportunity to write books and tour with Bishop T. D. Jakes in "God's Leading Ladies," where we speak at stadiums filled with tens of thousands of women. I am currently touring the country speaking on financial readiness and challenge at military bases. Some of my other career highlights include speaking to women at an annual conference organized by Congressman Steny

Hoyer, now the House Democratic majority leader, and I've joined several national tours for Working Mother Media, as well as some for the National Association of Securities Dealers (NASD) Office on Individual Investors.

For all these events, I view my mission as one of preaching the gospel of wealth building to women from all walks of life, whether they are the wives of corporate CEOs in Palm Beach or Walmart greeters in Niceville, Florida. Now more than ever, it is critical for me to encourage others to adopt habits and attitudes that will help them fill their purses in any economic climate.

I've talked with many women who assume that men make better investors because they learn risk tolerance naturally, but this is not necessarily the case. Psychiatrist Richard L. Peterson, author of *Inside the Investor's Brain: The Power of the Mind over Money*, says, "Risk tolerance is more a cultural or personal narrative that we tell ourselves." That means we need to learn to reframe our stories and see ourselves in a whole new light.

I'm not alone in realizing that women tend to be highly competent investors. Studies tracking men and women suggest that we are better than the guys at investing because we're more willing to collaborate with others who are more knowledgeable, including advisors and investment club members, while men have greater confidence in their own opinions. We're also less likely than men to abandon an investment when the price takes a dive, and therefore we're still around when prices do rise and we're able to recoup a bigger investment. In other words, when we do invest and tap into our formidable well of feminine skills, we rule. But we're falling behind because we're less likely than men to invest in the stock market. Women often tell me that they're confused and intimidated by the stock market.

The most determined women already invest. Others have resisted giving up discretionary time and income to master a subject that's presented as mind-numbingly complex. Since it's easier to grasp an idea when you can relate it to something in your own life, *Purse* incorporates commonplace terminology and everyday experiences to illustrate the point that finance-based concepts are neither complex nor foreign. As you shop for promising investments, your sense of style will inform your choices and your creativity and intuition will emerge as a potent force.

Purse can help check overspending tendencies by encouraging you to go to the mall to identify trends for investment opportunities. You might think, "I love that bag." Rather than buy it, you might instead gather information on which company manufactures it. Then you might conduct research, asking questions such as: Is the company public? If it is, how are the shares doing? So the next time you're in a store wondering about returns, you might not be asking where to get refunds on unwanted items, but about returns as in the profits on investments.

Seven of the ten chapters revolve around one of the principles of the 7 Wealthy Habits, and I've added three additional chapters that delve into subjects such as retirement planning and forming a Purse Club. Some of the chapters are also interspersed with "Purseonality Profiles," stories of admirable women I've read about in the news who exemplify the 7 Wealthy Habits. Where appropriate, I've included the exercise "Striking a Balance," which is designed to help you cultivate your female/male strengths. These various features work to support the ultimate goal of this work, to offer easy-to-follow, engaging investment basics, integrated into wealthy behaviors so you can undergo a Purseonality makeover.

I was committed to creating an investment guide for busy women that allows room for personal choice, and for that reason, I stuck purely to the basics in chapters one through eight, and packaged subjects that require copious detail at the back of the book, in the "Pursessential" section. These are essentials for your purse—just as a pack of Kleenex or tube of ChapStick are always essential in your purse—but only when and if you decide that you need to use them. In the same manner, once you master the basics and principles of this work, you'll be in a better position to decide how much more detail you need, and at that point you'll be able to turn to the appropriate Pursessential.

Purse utilizes a long-term strategy in which you keep money invested for five years or more so you can increase opportunities for gains. Numerous studies suggest that building a diversified portfolio over an extended period lowers risk levels. On the other hand, buying and selling investments on the basis of minute-to-minute price changes has been found to be very risky. You may survive and profit, but there's a greater probability that you might lose.

Purse readers with autonomous personalities may prefer to work through this book singly. Should you choose that option, there's a good chance you won't feel alone. As you begin to understand the process, connecting to a higher power might keep you energized. It may be helpful to use a journal to record your responses.

Those who want to use social interaction as a way of remaining engaged in this process may prefer working collaboratively in Purse Groups. These should not be confused with traditional investment clubs in which members pool their money. Purse Groups function along the line of the Weight Watchers' model. Purse Group participants offer one another support as they learn together and invest individually. If you choose this option, you will find suggestions for forming a Purse Group in the last chapter of this book, "The Sisterhood of the Purse." And throughout *Purse* I'll guide you to various websites. The Web has made investing available to millions of new-comers. Using it for investing is as easy as buying an outfit online.

Finally, I want to conclude by raising my purse to the women on the highway who used theirs for protection. Working singly or in a group, you, too, can protect yourself against life's unexpected forces as you learn to create a purse of your own.

ONE | GETTING TO THE BOTTOM OF YOUR PURSE BEFORE YOU INVEST

WEALTHY HABIT # 1: OUTLOOK

WHEN FORTY-YEAR-OLD LEE,* A MOTHER OF THREE, was asked what she carries in her purse, she was too busy to answer. She'd taken her two youngest children to the playground. Her nine-year-old was on the slide, refusing to budge and blocking his five-year-old sister, who was trying to beat him down with a Beanie Baby. After breaking up the melee, Lee returned to the bench to reflect on the question.

"If you'd asked me in the past what was in my purse, I'd have said soiled diapers and chewing tobacco, anything to deflect the question and hide my embarrassment." Lee understood that whenever I

---

*For the sake of confidentiality, I've changed the names and identifiable details of the women in this work who shared financial details about their personal lives. For that reason, I refer to them simply by fictional first names. The use of surnames means that the details of the individual's story have not been altered.

ask women what they carry in their purses, I'm not asking about the contents, but the state of their finances.

As a stay-at-home mom from New Jersey, Lee, who used to carry a purse running on empty, is unlike many women I've advised in the past or even those who participate in my workshops and seminars. To a large extent I'm in contact with professionals who work outside their homes. But I'm opening this chapter with Lee's story because at one point she was feeling powerless and out of control, and I thought her story could serve as an incentive to women who want to change their financial futures. I hope you'll see that if Lee could make it, there's reason to believe that you can, too. You may be skeptical about whether investing is a practical way to fill your purse, or if this subject will ever be made easily comprehensible. And of course you may be afraid of losing your money. I hope this work will boost your confidence and level of financial literacy, which I call "Purseonality Quotient" or just PQ.

The question of what Lee was carrying in her purse is significant because this chapter focuses on a symbolic kind of purse cleaning. It's not about throwing away wadded up tissues or old tubes of lipstick. It *is* about creating a more fertile environment that encourages growth, because once you get clear on what you do have, you will want to nurture and expand your inner vision. What I'm aiming for is to help you experience the kind of comfort you feel when your purse is so well organized that you can just stick a hand inside and grab what you need. Lee wasn't any place near that state of financial comfort. And if you aren't feeling comfortable with your purse, you aren't ready to invest.

She'd worked for ten years as a graphic artist, and for half of that time had managed a staff of designers. She quit that job, joining the ranks of six million stay-at-home moms, after giving birth to a disabled son. His medical needs made it difficult for her to return to the office, and her husband wasn't around to help fill in for her. His schedule as a fire fighter required him to work in twenty-four-hour shifts.

Not being able to work outside her home cost Lee and her husband, big-time. By 1990, the couple had saved $12,000. Eight years later, they were down to $2,000. "We were going backward," says Lee. Unable to afford child care that would allow her to work at a job, or to pay tuition to update her job skills, Lee felt trapped financially.

During a dinner with a former co-worker, Lee began sobbing so loudly that they had to leave the restaurant. She told her friend that she was pregnant again. "I was so scared I couldn't breathe," Lee says. When her friend pressed her for details on her finances, Lee didn't have any answers. Her former co-worker reminded Lee that she would never have run the art department that way. "She was right," Lee says. "I'd always run a tight ship. When I got home that night, I pulled out all out our bills and faced the truth."

How about you? Are you, too, feeling that your finances are moving in reverse? As Lee says of the state of her purse, "I was racing toward the bottom, but at least down there, there's no way to go but up." The purse solution offers an alternate route. Change your Outlook and you can not only look up, but outward, toward a better life.

GET ORGANIZED

Purse cleaning requires you to get organized if you're not already. This may entail making room for your financial documents in the drawers of a file cabinet or purchasing a cardboard filing box. If you need two drawers, fill one with papers representing income, everything from pay stubs to alimony; fill the second with paperwork representing expenses, from credit card statements to mortgages to child

WEALTHY HABIT # 1: A WEALTHY OUTLOOK

. . . .

This habit can help pull you out of the financial doldrums and encourage you to dream big by developing a macro or "big picture" view. Picture wealth as drops of molten gold. You may feel as if you've been living in scarcity, but because you are learning to attract wealth, you're now opening all your purses to catch those golden drops.

READY, SET, GO: START YOUR PURSE CLEANING!

. . . .

care receipts. Fold a page in half and on one side list money that goes out, and on the other, money that comes in. If you don't have more coming in than going out, you will want to figure out how to cut expenses and bring in more money, which was what Lee had to do.

After you've put your documents in order, write "Assets" at the top of another sheet of paper, and "Liabilities" on the other side. Under Liabilities, list your debts, and under Assets, list what you own, along with the estimated market value of these items. For instance, if you own a car, record the resale value under Assets, and under Liabilities, the amount that you might still owe on the vehicle. The accumulation of this information will help you create a net worth statement, an accounting of what you own and what you owe. Net worth statements are financial snapshots that let you gauge where you are so you can figure out where you want to go. The equation for a net worth statement works out to the following formula: Assets minus Liabilities equals Net Worth.

The summation of your assets might include the estimated value of bank accounts, real estate, cars, retirement accounts, stocks, bonds—anything you own that can be measured by a dollar amount. Your liabilities, are money owed on a mortgage, car, credit cards, bills, loans, taxes, etc. After adding up assets and then liabilities, and subtracting the liability total from the asset total, you will know your net worth. A free net worth worksheet can be found on my website at www.deborahowens.com.

This project may elicit powerful emotions. If you're living from one paycheck to the next, organizing documents can be akin to undergoing shock therapy—or not—depending on where you are financially. Women often say they feel shame about having so little or having "wasted" so much. If these feelings come up for you, take pride in the fact that you're working to change. If you're feeling anxious or angry, envision yourself hurling a Counterfeit Purse, one that looks good outside but has nothing of value within.

Putting together a net worth statement can motivate you to take action, because creating wealth is about adding to the purse. You will see at the bottom of your net worth statement in clear numbers whether or not you have been living a wealthy lifestyle, and whether you need to add to your purse. In Lee's case, the bottom line was worse than she'd expected. She and her husband were worth little more than $1,200.

This realization made her feel more defeated. Maybe that explains why she grew livid one afternoon when she was trying to vacuum before taking her son to the park. Her husband's feet were propped on the sofa as he complained about not being able to hear a televised football game over their son's noise and the vacuum. Furious and feeling overburdened, she ignored her husband's shouts and turned off the TV, insisting that they talk. She suggested that if he pitched in, she'd be able to find part-time work. She says he asked, "Waddya gonna do, rob banks while I'm home changing diapers?"

Lee was so angry that she turned the vacuum up loud and left it running as she slammed out of the house and took her son on a drive. Although she tried to think of a retort to her husband's sarcastic question, she didn't have an answer. "I felt like Alice in Wonderland after she fell down the hole. I didn't think I'd ever get out."

Many women are caught in this kind of dilemma: They need more money but can't find high-paying jobs with flexible or part-time hours. Once they begin raising children, many of the most highly-educated women have to settle for dead-end positions. According to Dr. Joan C. Williams, director of the Center for Worklife Law at the University of California's Hastings College of Law, women who work part-time earn 21 percent less per hour than those who work full-time. Dr. Williams explains that this U.S. part-time penalty is seven times higher than in Sweden and two times higher than in the United Kingdom.

Out of sheer desperation, Lee began cutting back on her family's expenditures. She squeezed money out of her grocery purchases, and served beans, rice, and salad twice a week, rather than more expensive meals. To save on gas, she drove less and walked more. In these ways and others, she saved five dollars a day, which she initially kept in a jar. For more details on how to cut back on ordinary expenses, increase your income and reduce debt, see Pursessential # 1 on page 213.

Lee paid off a high-interest credit card, and designed fliers, some of which she posted in the windows of local businesses, advertising as a freelance graphic artist. "I worked when my son was asleep. I never earned more than $1,000 a month, but I saved most of what I had left after expenses and taxes."

Lee split her savings between two accounts, one to build a nest egg and another to invest. "I was reading financial magazines and so many of the articles said that investing offered the only opportunity to really make money grow. I wanted to learn." Her husband told her she was crazy to even think about investing. She was about to give birth again, and this was during 1999–2000, when the newspapers were pumping out fear-inducing headlines about investment losses. A lot of new dot-com enterprises were going bust, and venture capitalists who had plowed millions into companies with unproven business models were losing money by the bucketfuls. From the outside looking in, this may have seemed like the worst time to invest. But Lee went ahead with her plans. She was only earning about five dollars an hour after taxes. "Investing was the only work I'd heard of that would allow me to turn a profit during a child's naptime. But I have to admit that I was afraid of failing. After a while, you start thinking of yourself as somebody's mommy, somebody's wife, until you don't feel you have what it takes to succeed on your own. I wondered whether I was smart enough."

Intellectual strengths are highly important for any financial endeavor, including investing. Lee was feeling so downhearted and ineffectual that she might have benefited by being reminded of the other skills she was bringing to the investment table. Maybe you could use a reminder, too, which is why I've developed a Purseonality Quiz.

The following twelve prompts allow for a range of descriptions. Please note that this quiz is not scientifically designed. It has evolved over years, based on feedback from a number of women investors when I asked them about skills that had come in handy in creating financial success, and which are not often recognized as such. After reading the prompt, please select the answer that comes closest to representing you, and circle the corresponding letter. No preparation is necessary; you only have to be yourself.

1. You devise solutions to problems.

   A. Usually
   B. Occasionally
   C. Seldom

2. You give to charitable causes or volunteer to help relatives, friends, and/or strangers.

   A. Usually
   B. Occasionally
   C. Seldom

3. You'd prefer a job in which you interact with others as opposed to working independently.

   A. Usually
   B. Occasionally
   C. Seldom

4. You keep in touch with loved ones with phone calls, instant messages, e-mails, and/or snail mail.

   A. Usually
   B. Occasionally
   C. Seldom

5. Sometimes it seems as if you can almost read minds.

   A. Usually
   B. Occasionally
   C. Seldom

6. If you saw a defenseless person being mistreated, you would defend her.

   A. Usually
   B. Occasionally
   C. Seldom

7. When you're busy you try to do several things simultaneously.

   A. Usually
   B. Occasionally
   C. Seldom

8. Strangers often smile at you or engage you in short conversations.

   A. Usually
   B. Occasionally
   C. Seldom

9. People often compliment your outfits or other things you've put together.

   A. Usually
   B. Occasionally
   C. Seldom

10. When looking at a house or apartment you can imagine living there.

   A. Usually
   B. Occasionally
   C. Seldom

11. You prefer long-term love relationships to short and passionate ones.

    A. Usually
    B. Occasionally
    C. Seldom

12. You like updating your wardrobe, and if you can't afford much, you add stylish accessories.

    A. Usually
    B. Occasionally
    C. Seldom

Once you've finished, separately add up all the *A* responses you might have, *B* responses, and *C* responses.

of *A* responses: _____

of *B* responses: _____

of *C* responses: _____

If you have five or more *A* responses: You possess many of the skills embodied in wealthy women. See the list of characteristics on page 11 that delineate strengths that can help fill your purse and which are exemplified in the 7 Wealthy Habits. If you have five or more *B* responses, the strengths required for attaining wealth lie within you and will continue to be developed as you work through this book.

If you have five or more *C* responses, it may be that you're so busy that you've scarcely had time to do anything other than put one high heel ahead of the other. Or these strengths may have become dormant in you after discouraging experiences. As you compare your answers to the list below, reflect on how different your life can become as you create wealth and have the luxury of time to develop these traits.

DECIPHERING YOUR PURSEONALITY QUOTIENT

1. You devise solutions to problems.

   An *A* or *B* answer suggests that you're creative.

2. You give to charitable causes or volunteer to help relatives, friends, and/or strangers.

   An *A* or *B* answer suggests that you're generous.

3. You'd prefer a job in which you interact with others as opposed to working independently.

   An *A* or *B* suggests that you're cooperative and social.

4. You keep in touch with loved ones via phone calls, instant messages, e-mails, and/or snail mail.

   An *A* or *B* answer suggests that you're communicative.

5. Sometimes it seems as if you can almost read minds.

   An *A* or *B* answer suggests that you're intuitive.

6. If you saw a defenseless person being mistreated, you would defend her.

   An *A* or *B* answer suggests that you're empathetic.

7. When you're busy you try to do several things simultaneously.

   An *A* or *B* answer suggests that you're a multitasker.

8. Strangers often smile at you or engage you in short conversations.

   An *A* or *B* answer suggests that you're outgoing.

9. People often compliment your outfits or other things you've put together.

   An *A* or *B* answer suggests that you have a sense of style.

10. When looking at a house or apartment you can imagine living there.

    An *A* or *B* answer suggests that you're a nester.

11. You prefer long-term love relationships to short and passionate ones.

    An *A* or *B* answer suggests that you know how to commit.

12. You like updating your wardrobe, and if you can't afford much, you add stylish accessories.

    An *A* or *B* answer suggests that you're fashion conscious.

Regardless of your score, *Purse* will give you many opportunities to call upon the strengths you already possess and strengthen those that lie dormant within you, to help you create wealth.

AVOID THE GAP

I hope you recognized some aspects of yourself in the Personality Quotient test. Scarcity can cause us to lose confidence in our ability to transform our lives. And much like the majority of women interviewed in a Prudential Financial study released in 2008, Lee was struggling with what researchers call a "confidence gap." She understood what she needed to do to take hold of her purse, but she was afraid that she would fail miserably.

Fear can destroy your ability to create wealth. I'll always remember interviewing Robert Kiyosaki on my radio show, and the wisdom he shared with my listeners. Kiyosaki's *Rich Dad, Poor Dad* books contrast people who focus purely on paying the bills each week and retire poor with risk takers who use money to invest and eventually create financial wealth. As an adult, Kiyosaki changed his own attitudes about money as he became financially literate. As one of the country's best-known financial authors, he preaches the importance of owning income-generating assets, such as real estate, stocks, and bonds.

As much as I enjoyed talking with him, I was disappointed after one of my audience members phoned in to say that she had finally dredged up the courage to buy stocks but was still a little shaky because she didn't have that much, and Kiyosaki discouraged her from investing.

He said, "When you feel like you only have a little, you can't invest. You can't succeed at investing if you're scared." I thought he was too hard on this woman, but now I know better. He wasn't talking about her not having enough money, but the fact that fear dampened any faith she might have that she could create a successful outcome. She hadn't realized that the world is filled with abundant riches and that she could have everything she wanted. When you start thinking this way, you can charge forward as if you are acquiring what is rightfully yours. Keep poet Robert Browning's message in mind and make sure that your reach exceeds your grasp. Reach for more than meets the eyes, reach for the stars.

I can certainly understand that many people are frightened about investing. That's why it's so important to only invest money that you don't need to put your hands on for five years. That way, despite downturns, you have a far better chance to earn a hefty profit. According to New York University's Stern School of Business, from 1928 to 2006, stock returns averaged 11.77 percent over the long run. Despite the almost inevitable economic downturns, long-term investing is generally the best way to beat inflation and build wealth.

As *Money* magazine's veteran stock picker Michael Sivy writes, "Over time, quality stocks will return more than almost any other investment easily available to individuals." The stock market is like a club sponsored by business that will continue to grow into the future by earning profits. The good news is that you have a chance to join the club, no matter your race, age, or gender. No one can keep you out. Pick the right companies to invest in and you will essentially be hitching your purse to the stars.

Sometimes I run across an opportunity to invest in products that I recall from childhood. For instance, my mother has used Tide detergent for decades, while I usually buy what's on sale. She has often asked me, "Why do you bother buying cheap detergent? You end up using twice as much to get the same results as the more expensive one." My mother is not alone in her sentiment. Millions of other women feel the same way and they have made the manufacturers of Tide, Procter and Gamble, a profitable investment over the years. How different my mother's life would be if she had bought shares in Proctor and Gamble.

I'm not recommending that you buy this company's shares, which are units of ownership in a corporation. But let's take a look at why it might have been a good individual investment for my mother. Procter and Gamble went public in 1890 and over the years has developed and acquired more than 300 brands, including Tampax, Pringles, Folgers coffee, Dawn, and Bounty. Procter and Gamble knows how to develop and market successful products, and its rise in value as a company proves that. If my mother had purchased $1,000 worth of Procter and Gamble shares in 1970 and remained with the company, reinvesting her dividends, she could have built a nest egg of $250,000 to supplement her Social Security and small pension.

Or consider one of thousands of other success stories. When Walmart came to your town, you may have noticed that the stores were big, the staff was friendly, and the prices were low. Suppose you had instructed a broker to buy 100 shares of the company? In 1970 Walmart offered 300,000 shares to the public for $16.50 each. You would have paid $1,650 for your 100 shares. With money raised from selling those shares, Walmart built more stores across the country and eventually around the world. As Walmart increased its profitability, it distributed dividends to investors, and many reinvested their dividends into more shares. A thousand dollars invested in 1978 would be worth more than $599,000 today.

The investments that give you the opportunity to share these types of earnings are stocks. Not all companies perform as well as Walmart or Procter and Gamble, but most investors would be happy to find one that performs half that well—and many do.

A voice of doubt may be whispering to your consciousness, suggesting that bargains were around in the past but not available to-day. I don't believe that, but I understand your wariness, especially if you're reading this during an economic downturn, when corporate earnings are typically depressed. I hope it offers a measure of assur-ance to know that the market bottoms usually signal that economic contractions are about to give way to exhilarating new life. That said, let me say that I believe the U.S. economy is resilient and will continue to grow over time.

Purseonality Profile: Karen Finerman

A Woman with a Wealthy Outlook

Karen Finerman, 44, is one of the most successful women investors in the world. According to *The Observer* (London), when Finerman, the daughter of an orthopedic surgeon and a homemaker, was a child, her mother advised that if she had to choose between a successful man or a nice one, she should go with the successful one because she wouldn't be happy if she was poor. Finerman came up with a better option: She would become successful on her own. That way, if she ever did marry, she wouldn't have to ask her husband for money because she would have earned her own.

Her dream was to work as an investor on Wall Street which was, in the early 1980s, and remains even today, a male bastion. And not surprisingly, many women are turned off by the long, brutal hours required in Wall Street jobs, which leave little time to develop relationships. Still, Finerman moved from dreaming to setting goals, and at least one of them had to include earning good grades in high school. When it came time for college she applied to the institution that topped the list in her chosen field: the University of Pennsylvania's Wharton School of Business. Finerman was accepted, and graduated in 1987 with $1,000 to her name.

Her next goal, of getting hired by a Wall Street firm, was quickly accomplished. She worked as an investor for nearly six years, and when she had enough experience under her belt, she was ready to play with the big boys. In 1992, Finerman and a male business partner founded Metropolitan Capital Advisors, a hedge fund, which is a private group of superrich investors gambling in high-stakes ventures.

As president of Metropolitan, Finerman's highly stressful job requires her to keep up with round-the-globe market movements. She seems passionate about her work and she has suggested that thinking like a woman has given her a certain advantage in the financial world, because she is not too proud to back up and admit when she's going in the wrong direction. She told a writer from *The Observer:* "A lot of men have a little bit more hubris, and I think humility is very important in being a good investor." She added that she's willing to tell others, "I had a thesis, but it's not working out the way I thought."

She adds that she can admit, "Maybe I'm just wrong."
At that point, she concluded, she would cut her losses
and get out.

That humility and knowing when to fold has
proven advantageous. Finerman and her partner started
Metropolitan with $4 million. Fifteen years later, it
was worth $400 million—and according to Finerman,
$100 million of that belonged to her. A full purse
means never having to ask your husband for a cent,
and Finerman said that she doesn't. Chances are that
her husband of sixteen years, Lawrence Golub, doesn't
borrow from her, either. He manages a private equity
fund (which differs from a hedge fund by investing
primarily in stocks). The couple has four children, two
sets of twins, including three boys and a girl. Finerman
described her husband as "very, very involved in their
schedules."

In addition to taking short family vacations, she
said that she makes it a point to join them from six
to nine most evenings, in the hours leading up to
bedtime. Once the kids are asleep she's likely to tune
in to *Bloomberg Financial* to check in on the overseas
markets. Although rarely away from family and work,
she said she celebrated her fortieth birthday by taking
four women friends she has known since kindergarten
on a trip to London. Finerman is also active in
raising money to find a cure for Parkinson's disease.
It's difficult to imagine anyone juggling so many
responsibilities. But then again, like the most successful

of investors, Finerman seems to have struck a balance between taking risks and taking control.

Finerman's Wealthy Outlook informs the way she perceives situations and responds to them. Wealthy women balance immediate needs with future goals. You can develop a Wealthy Outlook by visualizing the world as your oyster and giving yourself license to pursue your dreams. The very thought of getting everything you want may sound frightening.

A Purseonality Assessment

Finerman's story can remind you to:

Accept no restrictions. Even as a teenager, she rejected the Prince Charming myth and the idea that someone would rescue her. She didn't rule out relationships, but didn't depend on one for survival. Finerman also refused to accept that she'd have to choose between a kind man and a successful one. Those may have been her mother's choices but they were not hers. I hope you will also reject the damaging belief that having the right mate equals financial security. To marry for money, for what a mate can do for you, springs from the false assumption that someone should take care of you now and always. This belief can only bear bitter fruit.

Define What Success Means for You. Finerman threw down the gauntlet. She would accept nothing less than her own success, which is what women have long craved. As eighteenth-century author Mary Wollstonecraft wrote, "I do not wish [women] to have power over men, but over themselves." Finerman wanted a full purse so she could exert power over her own life.

Leverage Your Strengths. Today, like wealthy women the world over, Finerman knows what she needs to be most effective. She has maintained friendships with women who add richness to her life. She views limitations as possibilities. She stepped into a field in which so many men and women are unable to thrive because of the tremendous pressures and long hours. Finerman knew her strengths, and certainly flexibility is one of them, which is why she can back up and admit when she's wrong. Flexibility allowed her to adapt to the needs of her family, marriage, and job, and to make time for one of the most important aspects of the Wealthy Outlook, to give generously of her time and talent, which she does through her efforts in raising money to fight Parkinson's disease. At the core of creating wealth is the ability to add value to others. In order to gain, you must also give something of value.

WHY I'M BULLISH ON STOCKS

Despite inevitable downturns, the world will continue changing in ways that will allow you, a daughter, sister, mother, or friend to create wealth through investing. Here's why I'm bullish on the future of the market. Around the globe countries such as Australia, Brazil, Qatar, and the United Arab Emirates will experience stops and starts but will essentially continue to expand. Middle-class populations in countries such as Turkey, Korea, Thailand, the Philippines, Malaysia, and Gabon will surely follow this stop-and-start trend, but continue to grow nevertheless.

In 2007, India grew 86 percent in dollar terms, according to *The Wall Street Journal*. That same year, China's growth surged 59 percent. The country's gross domestic product was $1.3 trillion in 2001, and only seven years later had grown to an estimated $3.6 trillion. Since opening its economy in the 1970s, China has lifted more people out of poverty than any nation in modern times, and it is poised to become the world's third largest economy. By 2008 the Chinese had opened about 577 million mobile phone accounts, a number that was growing an estimated five million new accounts per month, according to Nielson research. By 2009 that growth had stalled dramatically, but I don't doubt for a moment that their economy will come roaring back.

Think of what all this means for an investing woman. Like their consumer counterparts around the world, members of China's emerging middle class will make lists before checking them twice, and will embark on a massive shopping trip. Demand will rise for toilets, towels, shower curtains, soaps, and toothpaste, as well as bedroom drapes, matching coverlets, rugs and clothing, backpacks and books—the list is inexhaustible.

Many of us women have been equipped by our experiences to figure out what items those shoppers will want. Surveys suggest that women consumers in the United States buy or influence the buying of more than 85 percent of all goods. We dominate the marketplace, influencing purchases of everything from food to clothing, cars to health care to home improvements.

Lee understood this line of reasoning, and her saving and investment accounts were growing, but she was still feeling timorous about losing her money. That's why she dressed up, took the train to Lower Manhattan, and signed up for a tour of Wall Street, or "the Street," a Manhattan thoroughfare and the heart of the financial district and investment community that has grown around it. The Street is home to many major banks, brokerage houses, and stock exchanges which are marketplaces for investments. The United States has the world's largest economy, so tremors felt on Wall Street rattle markets throughout the world. For the time being, the Street remains the global epicenter of financial transactions.

Before the tour ended, Lee asked her guide to snap a photo of her standing before the bronze statue of the charging bull, a symbol of Wall Street. A bull symbolizes an active market. On the other hand, the figure of a bear, an animal known for its ability to hibernate, represents a somnolent market when prices plunge. For Lee, the photo represented that she was stepping into a global community of investors.

"I placed it on my refrigerator," Lee says. "I looked at it when I was frightened, and I figured I didn't have to do it alone."

Here's what else she did.

- She formed an investment group with four other stay-at-home mothers so that they could learn together. Lee planned the dates around days when her husband was home, but members were welcome to bring children. They decided to learn together and invest separately. For the first few months, members challenged themselves to save $100 a month for stock purchases.

- She contacted the nonprofit National Association of Investors Corporation (NAIC) for free and helpful information and support on starting an investors' group. You can contact NAIC online at www.betterinvesting.org or by calling toll free, (877) 275-6242.

- After attending investment club meetings for six months, Lee decided to supplement what she learned with an online investors' education series. If you'd like to register for an online course, contact the National Association of Online Investors (NAOI). Founded in 1997 and based in Washington, DC, this organization can be found online at www.naoi.org.

Even during what appeared to be a precarious time to begin investing, Lee was able to use her investing skills to improve her family's net worth. Working an average of three hours a week to research companies and purchase stocks online in five years, Lee turned $25,600 into $77,000 after taxes. This translates into $10,000 a year, for an equivalent of working three and a half full-time weeks.

Lee plans to devote more time to investing when her youngest child is in school. She sure won't need a new professional wardrobe. She does most of her buying and trading when she's wearing a nightgown and bunny slippers.

Lee is hardly the first woman to use grocery money to fund investments. As a Detroit autoworker and her husband prepared for retirement, she shared news of a surprise she'd been preparing for quite some time. In twenty-five years, she'd earned $1 million in investments with money saved from household expenses.

But that autoworker wouldn't be considered unusual in a country such as Japan, where tens of thousands of homemakers engage in online currency trading, playing the markets, buying and selling stakes worth millions through margin trading, a potentially lucrative but far more risky course of investing than I recommend in this work. Although my approach may differ from theirs, they are operating on the same premise.

Whether you have a little or a lot, you'll want to look at investing as if you were starting a new business, which means, among other things, keeping good records, minimizing costs, and coming up with seed money.

Lee began by investing $100 a month into her club funds. Once she felt more comfortable in the stock market and had saved $1,500, she began purchasing shares on her own in Starbucks. She chose that stock because when she started cutting back on expenditures and missed drinking lattes most of all, she reasoned that if she was "addicted" to Starbucks, so were millions of others. If you had invested $13,900 in Starbucks in 2000, you would have made a profit of $6,100 in seven years. (While there's no room to detail every transaction in this book, I've used information from sharebuilder.com to give you a general profit range on certain stocks.) Lee earned more than $10,000 in profits from Starbucks. She has since made many other investments.

If you have relatively little, use your innate talents to figure out how to generate more. Lee and her husband's net worth had once been $1,200. Today they are worth $323,397. See page 25 for their 2008 net worth statement.

Lee's husband hasn't gotten any better about pitching in with the housework, but she does report that he's not laughing at her any more. Lee moved through her fear by developing a Wealthy Outlook, and you can, too. If you're unhappy with your net worth, turn your

ASSETS		LIABILITIES	
Cash in checking, savings, CDs, and money market accounts	$18,400	Apartment mortgage	$380,000
Retirement 401(k)	$73,280		
IRA investments	$196,717		
Apartment appraised value	$414,000		
Engagement ring appraised value	$1,000		
Total Assets	$703,397	Total Liabilities	$380,000
		Net Worth	**$323,397**

dreams into goals that reflect your desire to fulfill unmet needs, and plan for something better.

A PURSERCIZE: THE SUM OF YOUR DREAMS

Creating wealth is about adding to the quality of your life. When you value something and approach it with integrity, the universe will conspire to help you. This pursercize is designed to help you hone in on what you need to feel fulfilled. Many women I've asked included loving relationships, financial and physical security, a spiritual connection, good health, and intellectual satisfaction.

If your list differs, or you have more to add, please record your responses below:

1. _____
2. _____
3. _____
4. _____
5. _____

Once you've listed your unmet needs in broad terms, come up with concrete, measurable aspects of what you need to reach your goals, such as enrolling in a seminar.

1. _____
2. _____
3. _____
4. _____
5. _____

Now prioritize. Which goal should you accomplish first? Which ones after that? Record your prioritized list below, making sure to set completion dates beside goals and include cost estimates.

GOAL	TARGETED COMPLETION DATE	ESTIMATED COST

SUM: _____

How does it feel to see the sum of your dreams on paper? If you're frightened, use a soothing inner voice to reassure yourself that you have what you need to get where you want to go. Keep listening to this positive, loving message until your fears subside. Fear will rob you of the energy you need to create wealth. Remember the sound and tone of that soothing voice. Perhaps it reminds you of someone you trust.

You have reached a point in this work where you can reconnect with your dreams, change direction, and add new rhythms to your life. Taking a wider perspective also makes it easier to see where you fit into this world. As the world mirrors back your unlimited potential, you can see yourself as the extraordinary individual that you are.

A WEALTHY TIP

Speaking of moving forward, if you want to remind yourself of the importance of maintaining a Wealthy Outlook, start paying attention to the way you walk through this world. Your gait communicates to others and to yourself your level of confidence. Jessica Stam knows how to stride toward success. This supermodel struts down runways around the world and has so impressed fashionistas that designer Marc Jacobs named *my* favorite accessory—a purse—after her. The Stam Bag gives a new meaning to "a purse of my own."

Stam told *The Wall Street Journal* that she conveys confidence by walking with her shoulders pressed down, holding her head high and straight, and focusing on a point in the distance while taking long strides. It sounds as if wherever this young lady rests her feet, she views the terra firma beneath them as her very own. Now that's a Wealthy Outlook.

Striking a Balance

The female/male strengths of humility and courage were illustrated in Lee's story. If the spirit moves you, write about how you envision utilizing these or similar traits to create a wealthy life.

You may want to use some of the following questions as guidelines:

- What frightens me most about the prospect of changing my life?
- How has fear affected my financial life?
- What will it take for me to develop the confidence I need?
- How might my life change if I allow myself to act courageously to acquire wealth?
- If it's true that pride goes before a fall, how might humility help me become wealthy?

_____

_____

_____

_____

_____

_____

_____

_____

_____

_____

TWO | FALLING IN LOVE WITH STOCKS AT FIRST SIGHT

WEALTHY HABIT # 2: VISION

LYNNETTE, 36, A SINGLE WASHINGTON, DC, POLITI-cian and fan of my radio show, fell in love with stocks at first sight. Several friends told her they were "making a killing" on the market and she wanted in. She began investing in technical stocks in the late 1990s with money she earned from a difficult low-wage job while attending graduate school. Lynette's words sped up with excitement as she described what it was like reading quarterly investment reports. "This was a period when stock market growth was incredible. Every three months, it was like Christmas. I was reading and watching everything I could to learn about stocks. The flip side was that I was only twenty-three, so when I'd talk to guys about what was happening on Wall Street they'd give me blank stares."

Lynette hired a broker in 2000, when her share value declined by $3,000. He pointed out that she'd done well, given that her $10,000 principle had grown to $30,000. He suggested that she hold on to her shares until the values increased. Her other option would have been to liquidate her holdings and put her cash elsewhere. At that point, she would have come away with a $17,000 profit.

She took the broker's advice and held on to her stocks. A year later, it was clear that several of her tech stocks, such as PSI Net and Lucent Technology, would never recover. She'd jumped into investing so quickly that she hadn't learned one of the most basic, key strategies, which requires diversification. Lots of people ignore this advice because they fall so deeply in love that their emotions cloud their reasoning. It happens all the time. For instance, starting in 2008, lots of people who had most of their investment money tied up in real estate were wiped out when the housing market plummeted. No matter what you're investing in, never put all your eggs in one basket. I will discuss this and other strategies in the next chapter. In this chapter I'm focusing on investment basics, so you can start off on a safe and sound footing.

As for Lynette, like a woman walking down a dark alley carrying a bejeweled Prada purse, she was headed for trouble. But some people are blinded by love, and this seemed to be Lynette's problem. She had purchased mostly tech stocks and by 2003 she had lost half of her earnings. At that point, she closed her accounts and decided she'd never invest again. She says, "I learned that anyone who says they know what the stock market will do next is a liar. No one knows."

Even if you've never invested in the stock market, you may still know what it's like to fall in love at first sight. Affairs like these may begin with a shared glance and whispered words, or if the other person isn't big on conversation, it may be sparked by a mere insinuation of interest. Although ignited in a moment, your affair of the heart may feel like you're engaged in a life-changing connection. Suddenly bound to each other, you're reeling giddily and feeling breathlessly drunk with anticipation.

And then you get over it. Maybe your heartthrob wasn't the person you'd imagined. You might have noticed major character flaws or some unacceptable behaviors that proved resistant to change. Hopefully, you grabbed your purse and got the hell out of there. But didn't you find yourself wondering why you hadn't seen what was right before your eyes from the start? If any of this is bringing back old memories, I hope you are also recalling any misery you might have experienced when the affair ended. It's better to send you down memory lane now than to have you to travel the same path when it comes to your investments.

Love at first sight is a good analogy for explaining why so many people, enthralled by their emotions, become personal investors without ever figuring out who or what they're getting involved with. So let me make it clear right now: It's a given in the market that the greater the potential for profit, the greater the risk. That's why you want to skip the shortcuts, travel through the light of day, and choose safe routes.

Once Lynette learned the basics, she returned to the market with a different attitude. She now says, "You can make money investing, but there are no sure bets, so it's important to set aside money to cushion immediate losses. And you should know how to gather information for yourself. You don't have to be as savvy as a financial advisor, but you need to be able to understand what it is you're investing in. Regardless of what the hype is about a company, buy only what is proven, solid, and income generating."

If she sounds like a woman who has learned to make better choices about handing over her heart impulsively, you would be correct. Don't get me wrong, ladies. I'm not against love at first sight, but I've learned that a purse in the hand is worth more than two men with rings. The more a woman values herself, the more likely she is to look past surface appearances and take the time to ensure that her object of desire can satisfy her needs. It's the same for investing, which brings me to our next wealth-building principle.

WEALTHY HABIT # 2: A WEALTHY VISION

. . . .

Rather than taking the macro view described as a Wealthy Outlook, a Wealthy Vision encourages you to look inward and identify your comparative advantage, your unique gifts based upon a blend of innate characteristics. If you develop an appreciation of yourself and your strengths, you're more likely to get your investment needs met.

. . . .

To learn how to meet your investment needs you will want to:

- understand the difference between saving money in a bank and investing in stocks.
- remember that stocks have the greatest potential for high returns.
- consider your values.
- not buy into a company until you've done your homework.
- not let headlines scare you away from one of the most important relationships you might ever have.
- invest in companies that make products you understand.

Understand the Difference Between Saving Money in a Bank and Investing in Stocks

When you deposit money in a savings account, the financial institution invests this as well as what they get from other depositors into the stock market and other investment vehicles. The bank keeps some of its investment profits and pays savers minimal interest. This is basically a no-risk transaction, because the Federal Deposit Insurance Corporation (FDIC) backs each of your bank accounts up to $250,000.

The FDIC was created in 1933 after 4,000 banks shut their doors. Under the auspices of the FDIC, banks contribute to a fund to insure against losses and prevent runs. Before you deposit your money in a financial institution, look for the FDIC symbol, which is posted at every insured bank and savings association across the country, and on the websites of online banks. It serves as a reminder that no federally insured deposit up to the maximum limit has ever been lost to a customer.

You may wonder why anyone would choose to buy into a company, knowing that they might never recover the original amount (the "capital") or anything at all. They do it because there's a chance that the business or enterprise will repay them through an increase in value of their stock (appreciation) or in the form of dividends (income), which are how companies distribute earning to their investors. Since companies realize that folks would be far more likely to put their cash in a bank where it would remain risk-free than to hand it over to them in a more risky proposition, they entice investors by offering the potential for returns that are usually higher than can be obtained at a bank.

THE RULE OF 72

This simple equation helps you to determine a rough estimate of the length of time it will take to double your money in an investment. Simply divide the number 72 by the annual interest rate or return on your investment. Let's start with something supereasy. If you were investing one dollar and were earning a 10 percent interest rate, you would simply divide 72 by 10, which equals 7.2. This means it would take approximately 7 years for your $1 to double to $2. Now let's consider a larger amount. You have $10,000 and invest it at 4 percent interest. For now, forget about the $10,000 and stick with the numbers 72 and 4 (for the interest rate); 72 divided by 4 equals 18. It would take eighteen years at 4 percent interest for your $10,000 to double to $20,000. Now that you know how to use this rule, it will be easier to decide whether you want to invest your money in a bank, mutual fund, stocks, or bonds. Although your money will double eventually in any of these financial products, it has the best chance of growing more rapidly when you invest it in stocks.

Remember That Stocks Have the Greatest Potential for High Returns

You will hear many references to bonds, stocks, and mutual funds in *Purse.* All three are investment instruments that hold some degree of risk. Bonds are considered somewhat safer vehicles because when investors are paid off, bondholders get paid first and stockholders are second in line. Bonds are essentially loans made to corporations or governments by investors. With mutual funds, the deposits of many investors are used to purchase a diverse mix of investments.

Those investments are considered less risky than stocks. For the sake of learning the basics, let's stick with buying shares of stock, which has the greatest potential for high returns. A share signifies partial ownership in a company or other enterprise, and entitles you to share in the company's profits. When you invest in shares you aren't getting just a piece of paper, you're buying a piece of a company. Picture yourself walking through a busy mall or business district or driving past factories, mines, or manufacturing or technology concerns and pointing at some of them, saying, "I own a piece of that . . . and that, and . . ." As you can imagine, it's empowering to own stock.

Not all corporations sell stock. Those that do are trying to raise capital, perhaps to pay for the launch of a new product. Rather than use its own money or take out a loan, it may offer to sell a percentage of its company in stock shares.

When a company meets the Security and Exchange Commission's (SEC) requirements for selling to the public, the buzz is on. Investors hear about the upcoming sale, and if it's a big company with a long history of success, they line up to buy stock the moment it is available. Just before the stock is put up for sale on the open market, when ordinary investors can purchase company stock, the firms that participated in preparing for the stock sale offer shares to their clients—individuals or institutional investors—who trade at their firm. This kind of closed stock offering is like a "private sale" at a swanky department store, when top customers might be offered an opportunity to shop before the doors are thrown open to the public. When a stock is put up for sale to the general public, it is said that the company is "going public."

Let's say that the company has been valued at $25 million and is issuing a million shares of stock at $25 a share. Those privileged few get to buy the stock at $25 a share. Then the company goes public, or makes its initial public offering (IPO) to the rest of us. The more demand—people who try to buy the stock—the more valuable the stock offering is considered to be. Most companies never go public. They are funded by private investors or by the profits they make selling products or services.

Consider Your Values

When you fall head over heels about someone new, it's especially important to hold on to who you are and what you value. And it's the same for choosing stocks. I think that it's important to invest in companies that demonstrate that they are in line with our moral and ethical values.

To that end, you should know that there are several socially responsible investment firms that focus on companies that don't pollute, exploit workers, or participate in experiments that harm animals. To learn more, go online to www.michaelbluejay.com/sri/. Those interested in issues of social justice and the environment can consult the KLD Domini 400 Social Index, considered a benchmark for socially and environmentally responsible investing worldwide. And finally, Dow Jones & Company launched a Dharma Index in 2008 that tracks the stocks of 3,400 companies globally (1,000 in the United States) that observe the values of Dharma-based religions such as Hinduism and Buddhism. On the other end of the spectrum, the Vice Fund

Shares are sold through the "stock market," which is not a location but a term for the organized activity of trading shares at "exchanges." The largest and oldest stock exchange in the United States, dating from 1794, is the New York Stock Exchange (NYSE). Companies trading on the NYSE must meet stiff requirements for their stock to be listed and traded there. The American Stock Exchange is the second largest exchange in the country. Both of these are floor-based exchanges, which means they have physical locations. NASDAQ, the National Association of Securities Dealers Automated Quotation system, offers electronic price quotations. Many tech stocks are listed on the NASDAQ initially because they don't meet the stricter requirements of the NYSE.

In addition to exchanges in cities like London and Tokyo there are also U.S. regional exchanges.

Pacific Exchange	San Francisco, Los Angeles
Philadelphia Exchange	Philadelphia
Chicago Stock Exchange	Chicago
Boston Stock Exchange	Boston

(VICEX) is made up exclusively of companies that deal in tobacco, alcohol, gambling, and the defense industry.

The choices aren't always that clear though. Figuring out what's important to you in life can mean getting a handle on who you are. Buying stocks certainly helped Elizabeth, 47, an after-school program supervisor, in that regard. She and her family live on the fashionable Upper East Side, an area of Manhattan associated with the kind of wealthy characters populating the expensively costumed 2006 film, *The Devil Wears Prada*. But while that happens to be where Elizabeth lives, it is not necessarily who she is or a lifestyle that she values. In 1998, her daughter was just starting kindergarten when Elizabeth decided to try personal investing as a way of building up her own confidence.

"I was so nervous," Elizabeth recalled. "My husband was so encouraging. He's my inspiration. He didn't finish college but he worked on Wall Street, not as a broker but he did get to see how important it was to invest. He started before I met him, more than forty years ago. When I told him what I wanted to do, he showed me how to set up a brokerage account and we put $1,000 into it. But he didn't push me."

Through research, Elizabeth homed in on the Stop & Shop grocery chain. This store wasn't located in her tony neighborhood, but she'd frequented one in her hometown of Amherst, Massachusetts, and remembered the high quality, affordable merchandise. Elizabeth liked the company's hometown roots and that it reflected her values. The company started as a corner grocery and expanded to 360 stores, becoming New England's largest supermarket chain. Convinced that the company had good earning prospects, she bought forty shares at $10 each. It turned out that seasoned investors agreed with her assessment. Months later, Ahold, a European-based retailer, purchased the Stop & Shop chain and the share price went up $10 almost immediately.

She didn't make a killing on the deal, only $250. But she was as thrilled over this first small profit as some of her neighbors might have been at finding Manolo Blahniks in a 99-cent store. Elizabeth loved the idea of profiting by utilizing her analytical skills. She has since invested in Whole Foods and Home Depot, companies that she feels reflect her values.

....

For many Purse Ladies, buying stock may be our first opportunity to feel that our actions carry weight. I don't assume, of course, that all women share the same values. But I am fascinated at how investing can require us to look at ourselves. I hope you understand me well enough by now to realize that I'm not insinuating gender polarities, that all men are one way and women are another. I do believe, though, that because society imposes its constraints on men, many others are probably raised feeling that they don't have much freedom to express their principles.

As a result, some men who are trying to create wealth are less likely to feel that they have the freedom to consider their values, perhaps because of cultural conditioning. Men are taught that they're acting like wimps if they talk about what they value. Rather than complain, they're expected to suck it up and "man up." But that attitude has worked against the interests of investors and noninvestors worldwide starting in 2008 as unethical practices on Wall Street and worldwide financial capitals wreaked havoc around the globe.

Let's hope that once the dust clears, a more feminine spirit will prevail in the marketplace. MBA students at the prestigious Wharton School of Business are already being taught to identify core values and to express ways in which they're feeling out of synch with those values. The idea of bringing life values to the corporate world may sound like a dream, but I believe it's a sign of a better, more female-friendly world to come.

Purseonality Profile: JoAnn Price

A Woman with a Wealthy Vision

When JoAnn Price graduated from Howard University, married an attorney, adopted two of her sister-in-law's children, gave birth to a child, and continued working as spokeswoman and president of a trade association of investment companies in Washington, DC, she thought she was living up to her full potential. She might never have realized that her powers of persuasion could help her create a fortune, except for the fact that she remained open to new opportunities.

In 1992, she was meeting many minority entrepreneurs with great ideas and business know-how who were interested in building bigger companies. This got Price and a partner dreaming of raising money from cash-rich investors to form a fund for the purpose of investing in other funds that invested in companies owned by people of color. The idea of creating this "fund of a fund" excited Price, and she agreed to help recruit someone who could represent them.

"It was difficult finding someone committed enough to make it happen," Price said. After several disappointments, her partner suggested that she'd have to be the one to do it. "I said, 'You must be crazy.' "

He did convince her to try the job, though.

Many a time Price wanted to kick herself for saying

yes. During some seemingly never-ending days, she had to fly all over and try to convince pension managers to invest in her company's fund. They were usually white men, accustomed to dealing with people like themselves, and often wound up staring at her with blank faces.

"To their credit, they listened," says Price. "But most of those men didn't really believe that people of color could succeed. They were afraid to invest their money."

She spent another two and a half years trying to convince these mangers to give her company a try. "At one point I thought, 'This isn't going to happen.' I thought about what failure would feel like. It would be very public, because after all, we were a first. I couldn't blame the pension managers. If I allowed myself to become bitter or resentful, it wasn't going to happen. This was about taking a risk with other peoples' money. I had to be patient and allow them to go through the process of getting accustomed to me."

From time to time, someone would offer advice about how her company could better position itself, and she incorporated some of what she learned in her spiel.

"Thank goodness I was humble enough to accept advice when it was offered," she says. After she visited some pension offices more than once, a few of the managers decided that her company was worth taking the risk.

"We were able to raise $100 million," Price says.

And she wasn't just selling empty promises. Her company prospered.

Today, Fairview Capital has twenty-one employees, including six partners. With company holdings of $2.5 billion, her firm is a force to be reckoned with in the field of minority venture capital investing. The partners, including Price, invest in funds that invest in a cross section of companies, including radio satellites, telecommunications, and others specializing in the field of life sciences. In 2006, Fairfield was named *Black Enterprise*'s number one private equity fund.

With her children grown, a solid marriage, and time to devote to the philanthropic foundation her company established to fund efforts that include a summer camp, an arts program, and helping renovate the famed Apollo Theater, Price could easily pass her life off as near-perfect. But the earnestness that helped her convince skeptical pension fund managers to show her the money keeps her from pretending that she's someone she not.

Besides, she doesn't want anyone thinking that money buys happiness. "Reality keeps your life balanced," she says, and points out that two of her children have struggled with mental health issues. "Nothing in life is guaranteed. Nothing's promised," Price says. "You have to find peace and joy in the cards you've been dealt. I am so blessed, appreciative, and grateful for my faith. I'm not sure if I would have been able to keep knocking on doors without it." She believes that investing holds great opportunities for women. "I don't think we're as afraid of risk as men because we learn to deal with rejection. We're nimble."

Asked to share advice with investment novices, Price says: "Don't let negative energy enter your airspace. It can divert you from your goals. Find two or three people whom you really respect and who encourage your efforts. Set them up along your path so they can cheer you on and give you advice when you ask for it. My mother is my biggest cheerleader. She has no objectivity, and I love that. Everybody needs a cheerleader."

Purseonality Assessment

Price's story can remind you to:

Assemble Your Own Cheering Squad. Price limits negative messages by discounting hurtful unsolicited advice. She is grateful for advice from her husband, partners, and other people whom she trusts. If you've assembled a chorus of naysayers, they may reflect the way you see yourself. One way to start changing a negative self-view is to alter the lineup of people around you, by spending more time with those who champion your strengths. Think about how good you feel after a conversation with supportive friends and family. For those working in Purse Groups, this is a wonderful opportunity for members to reflect on strengths that you see in one another.

Don't Tell Yourself You're Too Busy to Become Successful. Price could have come up with any number of legitimate excuses about why she wasn't going to be able to raise $100 million to start Fairview's equity fund, including family pressure, physical exhaustion, and certainly the fact that she was trying to make her case to people on the other side of a cultural divide. Her Wealthy Vision allowed her to see them and herself as working together eventually, and it came to fruition. This doesn't mean you should always think positively; that's impossible and self-damaging, because it requires you to deny how you feel. Price experienced periods of doubt, but kept going until she succeeded, just as you can.

Picture Yourself Front and Center. Although reluctant initially to take the lead, Price stepped up to the plate. A Wealthy Vision allowed her to expand the way she saw herself. What about you? You might need to give yourself permission to act in ways that others might describe as "pushy." People who frown on women taking the initiative have narrow views about the importance of acting "ladylike." When opportunity knocks, see it for what it is and *purse-sue* it.

Don't Buy Into a Company Until
You've Done Your Homework

Researching a company used to take a lot more time than it does now. When I began my career as a broker, the firm would provide internal research reports on companies that were available only to our clients. Our staff had access to research from outside firms and had subscriptions to all the major research companies such as Standard & Poors, Value Line, and Morningstar. One of the allures of having an account with a brokerage firm was access to the information that their analysts provided on companies.

After leaving the investment industry, I didn't have full access to research and it wasn't as easy as it is now to find information for free on the Internet. For that reason, I couldn't act quickly when I first thought about buying into Coach Leatherware. Anyone who knows me understands that I have a particular fondness for Coach purses. They were among the first gifts given to me by my husband, Terry, who's still anchoring at Baltimore's ABC-TV affiliate. Terry was often at a loss as to what to give me, because I'm not easy to please. In fact, he and our two children, Olivia and Brandon, started calling me the "Take-Back Queen." They felt I was seldom convinced that we were getting our money's worth for gifts—unless it was a Coach bag. So predictably, for many Christmases in a row, Terry had a new Coach bag waiting for me beneath the tree. As much as I love the company's well-crafted staid leather bags, when they began to look stylistically generic, my latest Coach purse found its way to the return pile.

Then in 2000, I was coveting a friend's pink canvas Coach purse, and dropped hints to Terry that I'd like one of my own. When he finally got the message and bought me one, I loved the bag's girly-giddiness, and on some level of my brain I realized that the style change signaled that Coach had become more aggressive and competitive. I intended to check out the performance of the stock and perhaps invest in it, but I didn't follow up and I let the thought go by. Imagine my surprise years later when I discovered that it was that same year Coach went public at $16 a share.

If I had invested $1,000 in Coach in 2001, it would have grown to $15,000 in seven years, an average annual return of 200 percent. To this day, my Coach purse reminds me that if I want to keep building wealth, I have to make the time to follow up on my hunches and find out what's going on with a company that interests me.

Today researching a company is only a click away on the Internet. As you become an experienced investor, you'll find favorite research websites. If you want to be coached on researching stocks, one of the best bets available can be found online at www.betterinvesting.org. This is the official website of the National Association of Investors Corporation. For a relatively low fee, you can join a community of investors interested in rolling up their sleeves and learning how to invest on their own or through investment clubs.

Better Investing's Stock Selection Guide offers a research framework that I find particularly useful. After researching a few companies, you'll begin to feel like a pro. In stock research, you determine a company's future health. You'll learn to cut through the verbiage of annual reports and plot sales figures and growth of earnings per share to determine whether a company is growing faster than its competition and the economy.

Of course, growth is the lifeblood of any company. If sales, earnings, and stock prices aren't growing at above-average rates, you may decide not to proceed with a particular company. The amount of debt a company carries and the amount of money a company generates are important gauges of the quality of its earnings and its ability to continue boosting dividends. You'll learn to look for companies that consistently raise their dividends, returning the most to investors. And if you enjoy getting a read on people, evaluating CEOs can be entertaining.

Just as with your own financial situation, it's not how much money a company brings in that determines its ability to make a profit. Managing expenses is what allows the company to make a profit and provide investors with a return on capital. You will learn to look for companies whose earnings consistently rise and who provide shareholders above-average returns.

If a company's profitability is growing in-line with sales and earnings, you may have found a winner. First, though, it's best to forecast future stock prices. If potential rewards outweigh the risk, the Stock Selection Guide will provide a recommendation on whether you should buy, sell, or hold the stock.

Other sources for stock research include free websites such as wwwMSN.com. The *Motley Fool Inside Value Newsletter* can also do much of your research for you at www.motleyfool.com. Many websites are extensions of brokerage houses that operate in buildings—"brick-and-mortar companies"—while others are solely Internet brokerages. A brokerage house is simply a firm with brokers who buy and sell stocks on behalf of its customers. They act as the intermediary for their clients and place trades on the stock exchange.

Here are just a few of those websites:

www.Fidelity.com: This is the largest discount brokerage and investment company, with a network of investor centers. They provide clients with access to research from independent companies such as Value Line and Standard & Poors.

www.schwab.com: Largest discount broker; founded by Charles Schwab; and creator of Funds Network, which allows you to choose from an array of mutual funds.

www.etrade.com: Online broker with sophisticated trading platform that is preferred by active stock traders.

www.sharebuilder.com: An excellent website for beginning investors that was recently acquired by ING Financial Services. Their "What If" tool allows you to determine what an investment would be valued if you had invested certain amounts over time.

Don't Let Headlines Scare You Away from One of the Most Important Relationships You Might Ever Have

Bernard Madoff, the financial advisor and stock broker who cheated clients out of more than $50 billion in investments and whose crimes were exposed in 2008 surely frightened untold numbers of potential investors from ever trusting a financial professional. It wasn't just the enormity of the amount that he stole, which was breathtaking in scope, but also that so many of his clients were superrich and highly successful, so it was hard not to think that if someone could rip them off, it surely would happen to ordinary folks. So I understand people being wary of using advisors.

But refusing to have anything to do with any broker or advisor is akin to someone deciding that she'll never date a brown-eyed man because a lot of serial killers have eyes of that color. Maybe you're the independent type who never needs financial advice. Keep in mind, though, that financial professionals keep their fingers on the pulse.

They get to know their clients and can make recommendations about what's coming up for sale, what's available, and what fits the client's budget, needs, and interests. They often have their own research available and can make recommendations about what to buy.

So rather than letting fear over the Madoff case rule your life, learn from this horrendous case. Although quite a few of his clients may have been brilliant leaders in their fields, that doesn't mean that all of them were financially literate or took the time to understand investing beyond the figure they read every three months on their statements. A surprising number of his clients also gave practically everything they had to Madoff rather than spreading their money around.

Most important, perhaps, many of Madoff's clients were drawn to him because they had been told that he was such a whiz of an investor that he seldom lost money in the stock market. I have to tell you that this is impossible. Stock values wax and wane—sometimes they are up and at other times they're down. It's the nature of the market. If you ever hear about a broker who has figured out how to generate a near-steady profit, you'll know this is too good to be true.

Take heart in knowing that you're reading this book because you are determined to understand the ins and outs of investing. Someone pulling a con would, of course, want to work with those who are uninformed or naïve. No matter how experienced a broker might be, you would never want to turn your purse over to someone without understanding where your money is going. Madoff refused to answer clients' questions about how he was investing their money. I'm not blaming his victims for their losses, but I am certain that they would want you to learn from their mistakes.

In general, you will find that financial professionals use a range of different titles, including financial counselors, advisors, planners, stockbrokers, investment advisors, and so on. These titles are not job descriptions. In addition to being registered stockbrokers, some of these professionals may also be available to offer advice on selecting insurance, or planning for retirement. Stockbrokers make investments for clients and get paid commissions on the products they sell. Many of the women I meet use brokers or advisors and pay fees for stock transactions; some invest on their own, while others do both. Should you decide you need help, trust that you have what it takes to do the research and find a trustworthy financial advisor.

I usually tell women to steer clear of brokers or advisors who are making a pitch just to drum up clients. You aren't looking for someone who wants to sell you financial products. You need advice that's offered to meet your needs. Brokerage firms and other investment companies are required to register with the Securities and Exchange Commission, and they must join the Securities Investor Protection Corporation (SIPC), an independent organization established by Congress in 1970. This way, if the brokerage house or other insured firm fails, your assets would be covered up to $500,000.

The best way to find a good advisor is to ask for recommendations from financially savvy friends, family members, and colleagues. But a recommendation is not enough. Aim for four names and then narrow down your list. Once you get a list of brokers, do a background check by going online to www.finra.org/investors and clicking under "Protect Yourself" to the FINRA BrokerCheck tool, or phone (800) 289-9999. FINRA, the Financial Industry Regulatory Authority, a nonprofit organization, is the largest independent securities regulator, and is responsible for oversight of securities firms and stockbrokers, including employment and exam history. Their website tool discloses whether individuals have been sued or had consumer complaints lodged against them. You can also check at www.adviserinfo.sec.gov to see whether the broker has been the subject of any disciplinary action in the last decade with the Securities and Exchange Commission.

Before you agree to an appointment with a financial professional, ask what kind of agreement you would be expected to sign. Question this broker also about advisory fees, as well as the costs for buying and selling stocks. How you are expected to pay is significant; there's a difference between *fee-based* and *fee-only* advisors. *SmartMoney*'s Janet Paskin writes: "Fee-based advisors derive their income from a mix of fees and commissions; fee-only planners take no commissions. Conventional wisdom suggest that fee-only planners have fewer conflicts, but that may limit access to certain investments. Average management fees range from 0.8 to 1.5 percent per year."

Inquire about the broker's areas of specialization, explain your financial goals, and ask questions about how this person might be able to help you. Don't accept vague answers. Ask which experiences prepared this broker to work in her field of expertise.

You'll want to be informed about procedure, too, so you'll know whether you will be working directly with this broker or an assistant. Ask also how you would monitor your account with this broker. Will the broker monitor your account or is that your responsibility? When will you receive statements and stock recommendations? If the broker shows impatience with your questions, this is probably not the right person for you. And once you've engaged a broker, keep lines of communication open.

You'll find more details about hiring an investment professional in Pursessential # 2 on page 217.

Alexander Elder, a psychologist who researches investment behaviors, explains that women's knack for investing may be tied to our strong verbal skills. He has found that women are more likely to ask difficult questions, while men like to prove that they can handle pain, "and that's what gets them into trouble," says Elder. So don't be afraid of sounding "too pushy."

Invest in Companies That Make Products You Understand

Remaining within one's circle of competence is tremendously important in investing. That's a lesson thirty-year-old geological engineer Lois Boxhill of Vancouver, British Columbia, learned the hard way. She purchased AT&T shares in 1999, when many investors believed that anything associated with technology or telecommunications was a "sure" bet. Remember what you've read so far about sure bets: They don't exist.

Although she was unfamiliar with the telecommunications field, Boxhill purchased shares at inflated rates. When the telecommunications bubble burst, AT&T stock declined more than 30 percent and she lost approximately $500.

Boxhill refused to be stymied. She reasoned that her work as a mining administrator was the perfect preparation for—you've got it—investing in mining operations. But before she invested another cent, she delved into more research. "I read the mining news to find out who's buying what and to keep an eye out for coming trends," Boxhill says. "Some would think that's obsessive, but I want to know what's going on, and as a result my comfort level with investing has increased."

Boxhill also gets investing tips from a former colleague who has since become a stock analyst, and she reads financial magazines with an eye on learning how the financial world works and how markets are driven. About 40 percent of her portfolio is in commodities, including gold stocks and foreign and domestic mining companies.

Rather than using an exchange such as the NYSE, commodities and futures are traded on futures exchanges. A future is an agreement to buy or sell a good at an agreed upon date in the future. The New York Mercantile Exchange (NYMEX) is best known for trading energy and metals. This is where silver, gold, copper, platinum, oil, and natural gas is traded. The Chicago Board of Trade (CBOT) is where commodities such as corn, wheat, soy, soybean oil, pork bellies, and rice, as well as treasury notes and bonds, are traded. These are very active markets where traders execute trades daily.

Keeping in mind the importance of never putting her *bling* in one purse, Boxhill keeps her investments diversified by looking into other areas that interest her and that she understands. She is interested in blue chip companies—which means those that are well established and have a history of operating profitably through economic downturns.

It's important to digress here and tell you more about blue chip stocks, a term you will hear often in the world of investments. If you can think of a product that you use today and that you recall using when you were a kid, a blue chip company may produce it. In a poker game, blue chips are the ones with the greatest value. Blue chip stocks are issued by well-established, financially sound companies that have a history of issuing dividends to shareholders even through economically difficult times.

Boxhill doesn't invest in a company purely because it's a blue chip, or because it has a woman at the helm. But she does keep an eye out for good investments in blue chip companies that are led by women. To that end Boxhill chose Xerox, under the leadership of Anne Mulcahy (who was succeeded in 2009 by Ursula Burns, who became the first black woman to head a Fortune 500 company), and PepsiCo, led by Indra Nooyi. These women CEOs have overseen profitable results in spite of inheriting big problems.

Mulcahy took the helm of Xerox in 2001, when the company was becoming irrelevant as customers switched to high-quality printers. Xerox was wallowing in red ink, as it was being investigated by the SEC for falsifying financial reports. But Mulcahy guided Xerox through one of the biggest turnarounds in corporate history, reengineering the company to focus on document management. Xerox's earnings have increased by 8 percent annually on average, with revenues growing to more than $17 billion in 2007. If you'd invested $1,000 in Xerox in 2001, your shares would be worth $1,600 by 2008, a return of 61 percent.

Indra Nooyi transformed PepsiCo from a beverage to a snack company, and after one year of her leadership, revenues rose by 12 percent. A $1,000 investment in PepsiCo would have grown to $1,120 in twelve months.

I'm glad to say that staying within her area of competency paid off for Boxhill. In 2007, she began earning average annual returns totaling 15 to 20 percent of her engineer's salary.

A PURSERCISE: IDENTIFYING YOUR COMPARATIVE ADVANTAGE

You may have noticed that identifying your area of competency is similar to developing a Wealthy Vision, in that both encourage you to identify your unique gifts. Please take this opportunity to ask yourself which among all your skills you do better than most other people. This is not a time to be modest. If you don't know, ask those who love you. Now please list those skills.

My Comparative Advantages

1. _____
2. _____
3. _____
4. _____
5. _____

Of the strengths listed, which do you most enjoy? Which of these strengths is most likely to help you generate income? This strength or strengths can serve as guideposts to your future wealth . . . It's enough to make a Purse Girl fall madly in love with herself.

Striking a Balance

The female/male strengths of adaptability and discipline were illustrated in JoAnn Price's story. If the spirit moves you, write about how you envision utilizing these or similar traits to create a wealthy life.

You may want to use some of the following questions as guidelines:

- What situation do I need to adapt to or change if I want to create wealth?
- When have I been most adaptable in my lifetime and how did that improve my life?
- What disciplines do I need to establish to create wealth and how can I best do that?
- Who is the most disciplined and adaptable person I know and how might I emulate him or her?

_____

_____

_____

_____

_____

_____

_____

_____

_____

_____

THREE | USING WHAT YOU KNOW
ABOUT DIETS TO INVEST

WEALTHY HABIT # 3: APPETITE

IN THE SPRING OF 2008, A NUTRITIONAL STUDY THAT debunked the need to drink eight 8-ounce glasses of water a day fueled a national debate. Some people used the study results as an excuse to stop downing so much of the wet stuff, but not me. I got into the habit of drinking half a gallon of water a day after I heard that it helps control weight. Diet expert the late Dr. Robert Atkins believed that drinking extra water helps people feel fuller and makes the body retain less fluid. I know that when I drink plenty of H_2O I'm less likely to try to quench my thirst with sugary drinks that pack on pounds.*

I keep an eye out for sensible diets. I'm not into bizarre weight-loss fads, like the eyeglasses that purportedly project an image onto

---

* Please note that I am not endorsing any diet in these pages. If you're trying to lose weight, please check with your physician for advice.

the retina to suppress the appetite, or those stud earrings that are supposed to control hunger at acupuncture points. I have tried a few diets in my lifetime, though, and maybe you have, too. But no matter how much I may work to control my weight, the one thing I don't want to lose is my appetite.

WEALTHY HABIT # 3: A WEALTHY APPETITE

. . . .

Hunger from the purse standpoint is an interior drive for something that remains with you and affects the way you see your environment. When you crave wealth, you don't ever get too busy to pursue it. A Wealthy Appetite can help us stay motivated and continue looking for opportunities.

. . . .

Think about how you feel when you're hungry for food. You may walk past a pastry shop every day without noticing it, but when you're hungry you may catch yourself pressing your face to the bakery window.

The way we hunger as humans separates us from other species. To me, the expression, "you eat like a bird," reminds me that for birds, hunger is simply connected to a biological instinct. It's not the same for people, because we don't simply hunger for things. We become filled with desire, which involves a conscious understanding of appetite, followed by the intention to fulfill the need. When we hunger for something it's difficult to curb the appetite. And, in fact, stock market guru Warren Buffet maintains that both dieting and investing are emotional endeavors that require the need for self-discipline. This chapter builds on that idea, connecting what you may know about diets to develop the mental discipline to become a great investor.

Buffet, 79, the chair and CEO of the Omaha, Nebraska, Berkshire Hathaway, feeds his appetite. This junk-food lover puts his money where his mouth is, and invests in companies good enough to eat: Coca-Cola, Dairy Queen, Kraft Foods, and See's Candies. Buffett's portfolio expanded in 2008 when Mars, maker of M&Ms, Snickers, Starbursts, and Skittles merged with the Wm. Wrigley Jr. Co., maker of Juicy Fruit and Orbit gums. Buffett wasn't just whetting his appetite. Many of his investments yield sweet rewards and his stockholders often look forward to his company's quarterly reports.

Quarterly profit reports of publicly held companies are important to investors because they signal that the board of directors will be announcing how much of that money will be retained for research and development and how much will go for shareholder dividends. Dividends are either paid in cash (checks) or, if a shareholder has signed up for a dividend reinvestment plan (DRIP), the dividend will be used to purchase more shares so the investor's dividends can compound.

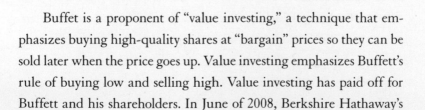

Buffet is a proponent of "value investing," a technique that emphasizes buying high-quality shares at "bargain" prices so they can be sold later when the price goes up. Value investing emphasizes Buffett's rule of buying low and selling high. Value investing has paid off for Buffett and his shareholders. In June of 2008, Berkshire Hathaway's

Class A shares (BRKA) were priced at a whopping $129,400. Buffet himself has an estimated net worth of more than $50 billion, and he is one of the richest people on the planet. In forty-two years of investing he has realized annual gains of 21 percent, more than double the Standard & Poor 500's.

> Just as you might check your pulse after jogging to get a quick read on your heart, the S&P 500 and the Dow Jones Industrial Average are two of the pulses of the market, indicating whether prices are up or down. Investors want to know *on the average* whether the companies in the stock market are increasing or declining in value. The companies that are used in this averaging are called "indicators." The publicly held companies that make up the S&P 500 and Dow Jones are chosen to represent the whole of market offerings.

Although Buffett can buy pretty much anything he desires, he has bequeathed the bulk of his fortune to a foundation run by his good friends Bill and Melinda Gates of Microsoft fame. His money will help fund education for underprivileged college-bound high school seniors, help improve U.S. libraries and high schools, and support a worldwide effort to fight malaria, HIV/AIDs, and tuberculosis.

As Dharma spiritual leader Ken Wilber has pointed out, "Men at high levels of development are really able to manifest qualities that are the greatest gifts of the feminine. This is when conventional stereotypes begin to fall away."

In a frenetic world of finance, Buffett balances male strengths (he's analytical, aggressive, and competitive) with female strengths (he's generous, humble, compassionate, and forges close friendships) to brilliant effect. Despite messages that suggest we must act selfishly to become wealthy and focus solely on the bottom line, he stands out as uniquely human.

Buffett points out that investing and dieting are alike, in that they're both simple and yet neither is easy. What he means is that the basics are simple to follow, but only if we refuse to let our emotions derail us. But when have we ladies *ever* allowed emotions to interfere with our decisions? While the five tips that follow probably won't help melt away your love handles, they will help keep your purse in hand.

Keep Up Your Liquids

Just as liquids are important to flush toxins from your system as you diet, liquidity, is necessary for investing. When I go on a liquid diet, I'm not talking about grabbing a can of Slim Fast. In financial circles liquidity refers to readily available cash—the kind you keep in savings and money market accounts, as well as short-term certificates of deposit (CDs). Those with substantial liquidity can also look into brokered CDs. Purchased through brokerages, multiple certificates of deposit will allow you to spread money across several institutions and still qualify for the FDIC $100,000 account insurance protection. For listings of top-yielding savings, money market accounts, and CDs, check www.bankrate.com.

Building liquidity may require you to cut your expenses. If you haven't been saving money, I hope to convince you to reverse that trend. Let me tell you, the sweetest sound a wealthy woman can make is her purse snapping shut. Saving is not easy for most Americans. In the early 1980s, the U.S. personal savings rate was above 10 percent, but by 2006 the savings rate was running at negative 13 percent. Although that poor showing began to improve after the 2008 recession, too many Americans still live on credit.

It almost goes without saying that you will need money to buy investments, but that's only half of the story. You also need cash for the unexpected, so you won't have to sell your portfolio at a loss. A portfolio is a collection of investments. Picture a worn but favorite purse holding all your stocks, bonds and mutual funds—that's your portfolio. Filling your portfolio is a wealthy woman's way of turning a sow's ear into a silk purse.

Since the aim in long-term investing is to hold on to stock until its share price rises, you will need sufficient liquidity so you won't have to sell at depressed prices. When Shirley of East Palo Alto, California, the widow of a rhythm and blues legend, received a lump sum from a record company settlement, she honored her late husband's request and gave $10,000 to each of their two daughters to invest in the market. It turned out that one daughter cultivated an appetite for wealth, while the other had not.

Shirley's older daughter put her entire $10,000 in a number of investments, including Nordstrom, and she had no cash left to use as a safety net. After three years, she was frightened when saw the market value of her shares going down, and she needed to replace her old car. This is what Buffett was referring to about the emotional aspects of investing. Nervous about losing her investments, the elder daughter sold everything in her portfolio, which by then was valued at $9,300. Too bad she didn't have liquidity that would have enabled her to hold on to her portfolio longer. A year later, in 2004, Nordstrom shares rose 60 percent. She might have walked away with $14,000.

Her younger sister had invested $7,000 of her $10,000 inheritance in stocks, some of it in Hewlett-Packard, which a broker described as a "high-quality company" offering "steady earnings." She put $1,500 in a mutual fund because she liked the ease with which she could withdraw it if she needed it. That left her with $1,500, which she kept liquid in a money market account. Over time, this younger sister spent the $1,500 cash from her money market account on emergency dental surgery. Then she rode out the depressed market, watching the value of her investments decline and then surpass her original investment.

Eight years later, thanks in part to Hewlett-Packard's expanding global presence, the younger sister's $7,000 had grown to $18,340, and her mutual fund investment had grown from $1,500 to $2,416. She had spent $1,500 of the $10,000 her inheritance, but this younger sister's $8,500 had grown to $22,972. Her big sister started with the same amount but now she had no money left. Their stories remind us that "keeping up on your liquids" can help you stay afloat and manage your fears while your investments grow.

Start a Diary

In a study published in the July 2008 *U.S. News & World Report*, researchers reported that participants keeping a food diary lost twice as much weight as those who did not. In general, women who want to lose weight have to ingest less than the average of 1,500 to 1,800 calories a day that's required for maintaining weight (it's not fair that this figure is 2,000 to 2,500 for men). One explanation for the food diary participants' success rate is that recording what they ate heightened their awareness of how much they were eating, so they could cut back. You can use a similar approach to cut back on spending if you need to save more to invest.

A Purse Diary operates like a food diary. It's a show-me-the-money exercise that will help you identify spending patterns by tracking where your money is going so you can cut out the fat. Later, you can use this diary when you're trying to help identify companies that you're spending on and then consider them for possible investments. For more details on constructing your own Purse Diary, see Pursessential # 3 on page 230.

You will find that tracking your money allows you to keep up with your cash flow statement and helps you see the difference between what you earn and what you spend. This will help you figure out how much money you have to invest.

If you're sick of receipt clutter in your handbag, consider ordering a Purseket (www.purseket.com), a cloth organizer that fits inside your purse, or use a less fancy and cheaper coupon organizer. To keep track of expenditures, you may also want to use a small notebook you can tuck inside your purse, or remind yourself with stickies, e-mails, or messages on your answering machine, so you can record the amounts in a Purse Diary later. Some women rely on digital devices to track purchases and expenditures. There are also computer programs like Quicken, or the Web-based program Mint.com, which has received high praise from *Kiplinger's Personal Finance* and *Money* magazine. Mint can help you track how much money you have, how much you're spending, and how much you owe. Mint can also update you on your account balances and send mobile alerts on bills, fees, and low balances. These services are free of charge. But there's a caveat: The company makes money from advertising, so please steer clear of the credit card promotions and focus on the features dedicated to helping you save.

PURSERCIZE:
SETTING ASIDE MONEY FOR INVESTING

If you're compiling a Purse Diary, after recording a month of expenditures in cash, check, credit, or debit, you can figure out how much cash you have available for investing.

My income	$
Spouse's income	$
Other income	$

TOTAL $ _____

Then subtract what you spend from the amount you have coming in.

Total incoming $ _____

(minus)

Outgoing $ _____

What's left: $ _____

What I need to save from what's left

(work toward six months of overhead): $ _____

The amount I can now afford to invest: $ _____

If you use a notebook as a Purse Diary, you can keep yourself motivated by inscribing inside the front cover your reason for wanting to fatten your purse. Or try attaching a photo of one of your goals (a college perhaps, or home or business), or go on the Web and download a photo of a favorite contemporary role model such as Pleasant Rowland, who sold her American Girl doll company for $700 million in 1998. Or, if you prefer a role model from the past, consider Sarah

Breedlove, whose name might sound unfamiliar but is worth remembering.

Born in 1867, this daughter of former slaves surmounted a formidable array of barriers: At a time when racism was rampant and life threatening, she was a black woman with no formal education. Orphaned at seven, she became a widow and a single mother by the time she was twenty. A few years later, she began going bald. There were no black hair care products available that might be of help.

Rather than succumb to despair, Breedlove fed her Wealthy Appetite, changing her name to Madam C.J. Walker and founding a black hair care company; she became America's first self-made female millionaire.

You can find photos of both Madam Walker and Pleasant Rowland on the Web.

Purseonality Profile: Anne Scheiber

A Woman with a Wealthy Appetite

There may not be a more striking example of a woman with a ravenous appetite for wealth than Anne Scheiber. If she had come of age in the new millennium, her investment acumen would probably have made her a popular fixture on the financial news shows. Instead, when her Old World parents refused to pay tuition for anyone but their sons—not their daughters—Scheiber put herself through college and law school in the 1920s, according to *Money* magazine. Scraping together her savings, Scheiber gave them to her stockbroker brother to invest for her. This was the Great Depression. Her brother's firm went bust and Scheiber lost everything.

But she didn't give up. Scheiber had learned on the job that investing could give her the clout that continued to elude her. A highly effective auditor for the Internal Revenue Service, she spent years watching her mostly male colleagues get promoted while she remained in the same position. Scheiber wasn't standing still, however. While hungrily combing through the accounts of the rich and searching for tax dodges, she learned the secret of creating wealth. Lots of rich people got that way, she realized, from investing.

Retiring from the IRS in the 1940s on a pension of about $250 a month, she plowed her $5,000 savings into investments. For the next five decades, this woman fed her insatiable appetite by investing and reinvesting, through market highs and market lows. By the time Anne Scheiber died in 1995, she was worth $22 million. She donated most of that money to Yeshiva University for a scholarship designed to help women.

Purseonality Assessment

Scheiber's story can remind you to:

Stoke Your Appetite. Motivation can be a powerful predictor of success. The thought of paying for the education of one young woman after the next must have been tremendously satisfying for Scheiber, whose parents had refused to finance her education because she was born female, and she was later passed over for promotions, for what may have been the same reason. Rather than getting mad, she got even by trying to level the playing field for women.

What motivates you? Life is filled with many choices that can lead to multiple courses of action. Your response and the path you choose will most likely be determined by the extent to which you want a future reward. So find out what makes you emotionally salivate and go for it. It can help to promise yourself small rewards. For instance, if you've set a goal of saving a certain amount and met that goal, consider how you might reward yourself.

Challenge Negative Societal Messages. The media bombards us with messages that suggest men are supposed to take charge while women are simply supposed to take care. These messages can numb you, curb your appetite for wealth, and leave you feeling financially oppressed, which I refer to as "pursecuted." I urge you to challenge these messages in discussions (in Purse Groups, blogs, classes, etc.) or in journal writings. It helps to remember the determination of women like Scheiber, who came of age early in the twentieth century, when some medical authorities were actually warning that a woman's brain and ovaries couldn't develop properly at the same time. Like the wealthy woman she became, she ignored false boundaries.

She worked her way through school to add value to herself.
You, too, may have had to contend with discouragement.
Consider sharing with others any shaming experiences that
dampened your confidence, or record the details in your
diary, so you can move on with vigor and continue to stoke
your appetite for wealth.

Learn from Your Errors. After Scheiber made the mistake
of thinking her brother could do a better job of investing
her money than she could, and he lost everything, she saved
up again while learning her way around the stock market.
No one likes to be wrong, especially when it involves money.
But even if you lose, you can win, if you learn from your
mistakes.

Balance Your Portions

I'm amused when I hear authors of best-selling diet books touting
the advantages of eating balanced meals, including all the major food
groups, to lessen cravings and stave off bingeing. Their plans sound
similar to the advice Mom used to give us for free. But at least folks
seem to be paying attention to Mom's advice. A 1980–2008 study of
5,000 U.S. consumers found that the percentage of dieters declined
from a 1990 peak of 39 percent for women and 29 percent for men
to 26 percent for women and 16 percent for men. If more moms had
known to invest they would have likely dispensed similar advice about
the importance of balancing a stock portfolio.

To maintain a balanced diet, investors use "asset allocation" to achieve a mix of stocks and bonds and to keep it balanced. Asset allocation allows you to minimize risk by reducing investments that have met your goals and switching to new ones in an attempt to gain more. For instance, one investment might be going through a downturn, while another type is enjoying a banner year.

Numerous studies have confirmed that the way investments are divvied up—and then sticking with that mix—is responsible for more than 90 percent of a portfolio's performance. So the amount you earn in the long run depends on whether your portfolio is balanced. And this turns out to be more important than which stocks you select. To rebalance your investments each year, you can hire a broker, consult a financial advisor, or go online to www.Morningstar.com to use the free X-ray tool.

The rebalancing process begins with figuring out your time horizon: the number of years you have to reach a stated goal. For example, if you're investing for a fairly short term, perhaps to buy a home in five years, you might set up your portfolio with an eye on preserving capital, perhaps maintaining 50 percent in bond funds while keeping the other half in stocks so you can benefit from market rallies and generate growth.

Bonds, which tend to offer more stable investments, and stocks, which tend to be more volatile, work together like two friends who are trying to cover a long stretch of land, cheering each other on and offering support during some of the more difficult passes. Investments work in the same way. The see-saw activity, with one going up while the other goes down can offset losses. In this regard, maintaining a balance can help you reach a financial goal.

Someone with a longer time horizon, an investor who might have six to nine years to go until retirement might tolerate more risk and put 70 percent of her holdings in stocks and the balance in bonds and mutual funds. Someone with ten years or more from her goals might tolerate even more of the market's volatility and may invest more heavily than the others in stocks, which are more likely to pay higher returns than conservative shorter-term investments.

It is not unusual for someone thirty or younger to keep all long-term investments in stocks because she has time for the market to recover from downturns. As you work through *Purse,* you will learn more about creating a mix of foreign and domestic stocks, as well as those issued by small, mid-sized and large companies, and those that represent various sectors.

Sectors are industry categories that comprise different parts of the global economy and that allow you to target your investments. For instance, sectors include financials (such as banks, investment houses, etc.), utilities (electric, gas, and water), and technology (computer and software companies, etc.). Just as milk is stocked in the dairy section of a supermarket and ketchup in the condiments aisle, the products, goods, or services a company offers determines which sector they're grouped in.

There may be a time when a sector such as real estate is faring poorly (as it did beginning in 2007) while another, such as technology, is booming (as it did during the late 1990s). There are mutual funds available that concentrate on specific market sectors, such as retail or travel and tourism. Sandra, 33, an attorney in Chicago, says "Asset allocation means not putting all your eggs in one basket. I am not averse to risks, and I allow my broker to take plenty of them on my behalf, but I couldn't sleep at night if I didn't know that I've also got some nice old-fashioned bonds backed up by the power of the federal government and several blue chips."

Some investors consider balancing a portfolio, much like balancing food portions, as an old-fashioned concept. John Bogle, the founder of the Vanguard Group, an investment management company, and the author of *Bogle on Mutual Funds,* believes this attitude can be costly. He told *Money* magazine, "Asset allocation is the most important decision investors must make. It helps keep our counterproductive emotions out of the picture, assuring us of some profits when stocks rise and some protection when they fall. It also enables you to 'stay the course' through thick and thin."

If you're new at investing, balancing a portfolio may sound difficult at first, but keep in mind that riding a two-wheel bicycle might look almost impossible at first glance, but once you get started, this mode of transportation can get you far with minimal effort.

Trouble arises during rebalancing when advisors suggest selling winning stocks because they recognize the importance of taking profits in order to reinvest to take advantage of other opportunities. Financial advisors generally recommend rebalancing if you've strayed by five percentage points or more from your original allocation. To get back to the original mix—say, a 65 percent exposure to stocks and 35 percent to bonds—you may have to sell some winning stocks and reinvest the proceeds in bonds.

Be Prepared to Hit a Plateau

Sometimes you're following a diet religiously, and the numbers on the scale seem to lock into position and stay stuck for days, even weeks. Few things can be more depressing than hitting a diet plateau. This is when that little voice in your head tells you to go ahead and gobble up those potato chips, because you aren't losing weight anyway, so what does it matter? Hold on, Purse Girl! It may seem as if you're not making progress, but there's probably a whole lot occurring that you can't see yet. In other words, change is just around the bend, but if you give up now it will never be realized.

This same level of discipline required for riding out a dieting plateau can be applied to investing. Jean-Marie Eveillard, former manager of First Eagle Funds, and viewed as a top financial manager, told a reporter that "in the short term, the market is a voting machine where people vote with their dollars, but in the long term, it's a weighing machine that measures the realities of business." He's a value investor who understands that stock prices fluctuate daily as millions of investors follow herd instincts and sell when they get frightened by headlines or rumors, and jump ship, losing out in the bargain.

People who don't depend on the numbers on a scale or the numbers in the market to be convinced that they should stay on course have developed an internal measure that allows them to see value in what others overlook. Not following along with the herd, and trusting your own judgment, is an absolute necessity for successful investing.

Detox Your Purse

Some dieters believe that certain foods such as meat, sugar, some grains, dairy foods, and caffeine contain toxins leave them feeling sluggish and stressed and make it difficult to lose excess weight. Some follow detox diets that include fasting, followed by a diet of water, raw vegetables, fruit, and fruit juices. Although the famed Mayo Clinic has reported on their website that there is no evidence that these diets remove toxins from the body, and that "most ingested toxins are efficiently and effectively removed by the kidneys and liver and excreted in urine and stool," these diets remain popular.

While there may not be evidence to support detox food diets, I can tell you with assurance that detox financial diets in which you clean out your purse have been shown to have powerful beneficial results. Paying off debt before you start investing will give you the peace of mind you need to allow your assets to grow.

Paying off debt can be as difficult as trying to shed and keep off pounds. But if you're in debt, limit credit card use that, according to some studies, may swell your waistline along with your balance. It's probably no coincidence, for instance, that when McDonald's began accepting credit and debit cards in 2004, diners using plastic on average spent $2.50 more than those who paid cash. Also not surprising, "people eat more when there's more in front of them," says Ephraim Leibtag, a U.S. Department of Agriculture economist.

Reducing debt can lighten your load. A $20,000 debt can easily swell to $30,000 and take twelve years to repay. Imagine instead investing $30,000 over a comparable period and earning $100,000. Every dollar freed from debt has the potential to generate double-digit returns.

Another financial tactic for reducing empty calories is to boost your credit score. A poor credit rating weighs you down, costing you higher interest rates on credit cards, car loans, a mortgage or rental—and even potential employers factor this information into hiring decisions. Building a good credit record and freeing yourself of debts will empower you to take advantage of numerous investment opportunities that come your way. A credit score is a three-digit number ranging from 400 to 850, indicating your credit worthiness. The score is based on data about your history of paying bills, the amount you owe, and whether you've applied and been accepted or rejected recently for more credit. If you want to raise your score, be sure to pay your credit card bills on time and keep balances at no more than 25 percent of your limit. To get a free credit report go online to www.annual creditreport.com. For more information on reducing your debts and increasing your credit score, see Pursessential # 4 on page 233.

FOR THE CARE AND FEEDING OF YOUR WEALTHY APPETITE

Few strategies can help you reduce faster than a combination of diet and exercise, and of course I'm going to offer similar advice for improving the state of your purse. When it comes to investing, I'm not worried about working up a sweat so much as keeping apprised of changing markets. Success in investing requires that you continue to boost your Purseonality Quotient, and here's how:

- Read about investing at www.Bloomberg.com or www .CNNMoney.com, or in the print or online version *The Wall Street Journal.*

- When you find pertinent articles in monthly magazines such as *Money* or *Kiplinger's Personal Finance,* mark the pages with color-coded stickers, such as yellow for retirement; red for finding a financial advisor, and so on.

- You might enjoy filling a scrapbook with recommended stock suggestions from these periodicals.

- Attend investment seminars to increase your knowledge and talk with others who can share tips and information. And keep in mind that attending financial seminars is also a great way to meet potential soul mates.

- Listen to financial shows on the radio. And if you're in the Washington/Baltimore/Virginia area, listen to my personal finance show, *Real Money,* Tuesday evenings at seven o'clock, WEAA, 88.9FM.

Diane Hill, a North Carolina–based marketing manager who keeps an eye out for stock recommendations and devours financial magazines and books, says: "My television lives on CNBC." This habit has lined her purse with gold. After reading about a new offering in 2004, she invested several thousand dollars in Google (GOOG) at the company's initial public offering. At that point, shares were selling for $100 a share. Three years later they sold for $750 a share.

Finally, if you think wealth building requires a major overhaul of your finances, let me suggest that you simply start by practicing one of the tips I've mentioned above. Once you get that one mastered, add another, the way you might add different kinds of weights in a body-building class.

Striking a Balance

Anne Scheiber's story exemplifies the female/male strengths of savvy and decisiveness. If the spirit moves you, write about how you envision utilizing these or similar traits to create a wealthy life.

You may want to use some of the following questions as guidelines:

- How can I utilize what I'm learning in my vocation to increase my wealth?
- In what areas do I need to become more savvy?
- What are some examples of how I've responded to difficult situations with good old common sense?
- In what areas do I need to be more decisive?

_____

_____

_____

_____

_____

_____

_____

_____

_____

_____

FOUR | KNOWING WHEN TO HOLD
STOCKS AND WHEN TO FOLD 'EM

WEALTHY HABIT # 4: MINDSET

WHEN I HEAR THE PHRASE "KNOWING WHEN TO hold and when to fold," I think of a poker player developing instincts for when to hang on to cards and when to get out of the game. That fits with this chapter's theme, which is about knowing when to keep stocks and when to let them go. But in keeping with this book's larger message of ramping up your Purseonality Quotient, I believe that the most significant word in that phrase is "knowing."

Knowing, of course, involves knowledge, including developing a circle of competence and a mastery of investment techniques. And that book knowledge can be greatly enhanced when joined with what may be our powerful feminine strength of intuition. This triumvirate of intelligences can help us know when to hold on to stocks and when to let them go.

But could intuition really be of help in selecting stocks? For that endeavor, many financial professionals might advise you to stick to the facts and draw upon masculine strengths that lead you to be purely analytical and decisive. But you could find that advice in any old book. *Purse* is written to encourage you to depend upon your whole self. Remember the wisdom of Kristi Wetherington, the chief executive of Capital Institutional Services in Dallas. Wetherington eschews conservative bankers' suits and instead carries bold handbags and wears colorful dresses. When *The Wall Street Journal* asked about her unusual banker's style, Wetherington shared her philosophy: Do not be afraid to be a woman. I heartily agree, so let's begin by firing up your intuition.

Please don't underestimate the power of your "third eye" that allows you to see what you might otherwise miss. You probably won't be surprised to learn that intuition is considered so valuable that one Manhattan psychic, a single mother, is on retainer for up to $10,000 a month for a roster of clients including financial professionals. In fact, she went into business after a hedge-fund friend started paying her for tips. These days, she also instructs members of the Harvard Business School Network of Women Alumnae on how to use their sixth sense. This woman's success brings me to another key behavior.

WEALTHY HABIT # 4: A WEALTHY MINDSET

• •

Developing a Wealthy Mindset is about using your intuition and then following your dreams. A Wealthy Mindset requires a certain gravitas: spiritual heft and substance, a belief in your own strengths, and seriousness of purpose that keeps you hunkered down, no matter the opposing force.

• •

Few personality characteristics are more important to develop for success in the stock market than a Wealthy Mindset. It gives you the courage to buy and hold on when the herd smells a loss and ducks and runs for cover. A Wealthy Mindset keeps you going in the face of adversity. What others may see as a problem, you may view as an opportunity. Someone might suggest that something is impossible, but a Wealthy Mindset allows you to stay the course, like a ship on rough seas.

A Purseonality Profile: Helen Greiner

A Woman with a Wealthy Mindset

Helen Greiner, now 43, was disappointed as a girl when she learned that her *Star Wars* hero R2-D2 was just an actor in a can. She envisioned building real robots one day, and this dream was no passing fancy. She dug in her heels and earned both a bachelor's degree in mechanical engineering and a master's in computer science from the Massachusetts Institute of Technology, before cofounding the iRobot company with business partners, laboring in a workshop over a grocery store. This mother of invention and computer geek might have been grounded by her fear of flying and painful shyness.

But determined to see her dream realized, she fought through her fears and spent three years traveling and sharing her vision with venture capitalists. Despite fifty rejections, Greiner persisted until a company offered seed money to help expand their company to 500 employees. They have since manufactured and sold more than three million Roomba vacuums and 1,500 military-use PacBots to defuse bombs in Iraq and Afghanistan, generating $249 million in revenues. The iRobot Corporation went public in 2005, with more than twenty-three million shares of common stock priced at $24 per share. At December 30, 2007, there were approximately 24,448,000 shares of common stock outstanding.

When Greiner's former advisor at the Massachusetts Institute of Technology was asked about Greiner's days as a student, he said that if he'd been asked to pick which of his students was going to turn into a leading businesswoman, he recalled her extreme shyness and said, "I wouldn't have picked Helen." Asked about her transformation, he could only say, "She used her iron will to change herself."

Purseonality Assessment

Greiner's story reminds us that's it's important to:

Do What You Love. A job is what you do for a living, like driving a bus. With this kind of employment, the workday ends and you park the bus and go home. But a career can transform your life. If you love it, you'll be able to generate enthusiasm and fill your purse.

Become a Persuasive Speaker. Don't convey a lack of confidence by answering a question with a sentence that sounds as if it ends with a question mark. ("The answer is blue?") Another sign of insecurity is overuse of the word "like." ("He, like, used to be, like . . .") Valley Girl speech can destroy the potency of your words.

Capitalize on Any Shyness by Becoming a Great Listener. Greiner may be remembered as shy at her alma mater, but she learned to capitalize on her modesty by becoming a great listener. Whether you're highly conversant or tend to be shy, you'll want to learn to be a good listener. Famed psychiatrist Karl Menninger described listening as a magnetic creative force. It makes others feel that they're foremost on your mind. If your thoughts wander when someone talks, refocus, maintain eye contact, and if the situation warrants, nod in encouragement.

You will need to muster a great deal of resolve when investing in stocks. Holding on to stocks while the market gyrates can be excruciating, but that's the approach recommended by the most successful buyers. Buy-and-hold investors hang tough in the assurance that it's more of a risk to pull out of the market than not invest at all. They base that belief on market history. When measuring overall price movement, the S&P 500 barely budged between 1966 and 1982. But during that seventeen-year period, there were nine separate bull and bear markets. Investors who missed out on the action also missed out on the gains.

Women investors seem to understand to a greater degree than

men that trading stocks frequently works to the investor's detriment. As far back as 1998, University of California researchers analyzed more than 35,000 investment accounts and found that men traded 45 percent more than women. As a result, the men in the study earned annual risk-adjusted net returns of 1.4 percent less. A 2005 Digital Look survey also found women holding on to stocks longer, generated an 18 percent return compared to 11 percent for men during a period when the *Financial Times* Stock Index rose 13 percent.

Those findings highlight one of the most significant concepts you will need to understand as a long-term investor. Market prices rise and fall on the basis of factors that may have little to do with a company's worth. The stock market is highly reactive. Let's say that Walmart stock prices take a dive after a company official says something offensive on a video that's posted on YouTube. Demonstrators set up picket lines nationwide in front of Walmart stores, which spooks investors who fear profits will fall (which they might). The herd instinct kicks in. The need to follow the crowd is instinctual and can cloud judgment and make others more likely to ignore their own assessment and start selling, too. In our scenario, more investors join the selling frenzy and drive down the price of Walmart stock.

What about you? Will you sell your Walmart stock even though you might suffer a loss? The price per share may be less than you paid. This may be a good time to remind yourself why you chose the stock in the first place and trust your own judgment. Here are some other techniques for maintaining emotional balance.

Turn on your "slow-cooker" mentality: Picture your portfolio as if were cooking something delicious over time. Stock prices rise and fall from month to month. What is low in the present may recover in bull markets.

Be grateful for market volatility: Erratic market behavior triggers the herd instinct and prices fall, which means they'll be more affordable for you.

Think of volatility as a kid throwing a tantrum: Experienced moms know to remain calm when a toddler or teen (or spouse) throws a tantrum. It's the same for a cranky market. Remind yourself that this, too, shall pass.

Treat your portfolio as you would a loved one: Rebalance your stocks regularly and leave your portfolio alone. Don't pick on it or worry it to death. Take comfort in the knowledge that diversification works.

Nest: Mama birds settle in to give their eggs time to hatch. Doing nothing isn't easy, but as Warren Buffett says, returns decrease as motion increases.

Your brain is wired for panic, so turn off the alarms: If you're in a bear market, refrain from checking stock reports hourly. Researchers have found that the more people check stock prices, the greater their risks appear to be. Another study found that the more news investors get on their holdings, the more likely they are to trade and thus lower their returns.

Mount this information in a magnetic refrigerator frame: If you had invested in an S&P 500–index fund in August 1997 and held on to it for a decade, you'd have received an 88 percent return. But if you'd pulled out and missed the twenty highest market days in that time, you'd have had a 20 percent loss. If you pull out of the market temporarily, you'll miss the whole point of owning stocks.

We've talked about the difficulty of holding on to a stock to give it time for the price to recover and rise, but letting go can also be difficult, even for some who should know better. Karen, an investment banker for Lehman Brothers told me that she loaded her portfolio with company stock, despite the fact that most experts advise that a portfolio should not include more than 10 percent of your employer's stock (or of any investment). Karen says she held on to the shares even when she could have sold a great deal of it. She convinced herself that the shares would return to their fifty-two-week high of $67.73. The week after her interview, however, the bank's share prices fell more than 93 percent and were selling at little more than twenty cents a share. Lehman Brothers soon collapsed and Karen lost pretty much everything.

Another woman, Greta, a personal investor in Portland, Maine, held on to Ford Motor Company stock because her extended family had worked for Ford and were proud of their union membership. When Greta read reports that suggested that the company wasn't keeping an eye on the future, she still didn't pull out, and lived to regret her inaction. In 1998, Ford's shares sold for $32.32. Ten years later they were selling for $4.81, an 8.5 percent decline. In 1998, if you had invested $1,000 in Ford, by 2008 you'd have $150 left. This investor says she lost thousands of dollars.

It wasn't surprising to me to hear Karen and Greta express regret, as if they were describing romantic breakups. If you find yourself feeling that way about stocks you know should be sold, get a grip on your purse, girlfriend. Investing is a business, and business is about making money. Holding on to to stock that's not giving you what you need is as unwise as holding on to a lover who is unloving. Not selling when you should is one of the biggest mistakes investors make. They either pull out too soon or wait too long.

This advice may sound as if it contradicts what I've been saying about the importance of holding on to investments for the long run, but it doesn't. Sometimes we pick stocks that remain in semi-permanent decline, and when we see the error of our ways we've got to dump 'em. Your mission as a Purse Girl is to increase your wealth through investments. Holding on to stocks that devalue your purse flies in the face of this mission.

HOW MUCH TIME SHOULD YOU GIVE A LOSER?

Generally you will want to wait at least a year, but if only six to eight months have passed since you purchased the stock and you realize that it needs to be unloaded, figure out what went wrong so you can learn from this experience, and move on. Perhaps you bought the stock just before its sector underwent tumult, such as financials in 2007 and 2008. Or maybe technological developments have occurred that make the stocks you hold suddenly seem outdated, as with the demise of newspaper stocks. Or your reason for changing your mind might simply be that you've found something you like better.

Be prepared for reluctance on your part. As you saw from Greta and Karen's stories, letting go can be difficult, especially if you've invested in a company that earned your loyalty by churning out years of healthy dividends. I've often heard investors speak of companies as if referring to family members. But like mystery writers who create characters they love, successful investors have to be prepared to kill their darlings. Here are some of the reasons that may be holding you back.

You don't want to be wrong: Because women are expected in our society to be "perfect"—from the way we look to the way we behave—shame is a big issue for us. Sometimes not wanting to be wrong can lead us to make the wrong decisions. Sometimes the herd *is* correct.

You're afraid of losing potential future gains: You may have experienced a situation in which you sell some shares and then the prices seem to rise automatically. Maybe you're thinking that if you hold out, you'll be able to break even, or even sell at a profit. I say that when you know it's time for a stock to go, let go and don't get greedy, because that's when you will make mistakes. If you stew over how much you could have made if only you'd waited, you're creating a fantasy. No one knows how to time the market or has a crystal ball to see into the future. That means you'll want to develop a discipline and a process for selling, and stick with it.

You're too busy to sell: I see this as a matter of self-esteem. Emma, a retired social worker, told me she hadn't sold $6,000 in Boeing stock when she and members of her investment club agreed they would. As a result of her inaction, she lost $1,800. The other club members followed through on their ends and did not lose out. Emma said she was so busy helping her daughter with her new baby that she hadn't had time to sell the stock. For $100 she could have hired a baby nurse to help her daughter, and spent two hours reviewing her portfolio before selling her Boeing stock.

Sometimes we have to remind ourselves to make our own needs a top priority.

I've included information in Pursessential # 5 on page 238 on how to buy and sell investments.

CONSIDER TAXES

Before you sell your shares, consider whether you will make money on the sale, and if so, how much. If you don't know how this will affect your tax status, it may be wise to ask an accountant. If you're losing money in the deal, then that, too, should be considered, since you can write off losses. Short-term losses—stocks held for less than twelve months—can be deducted directly from income or can be used to offset capital gains up to a maximum of $3,000 each year (in tax year 2008). Capital gain is the amount that exceeds what you've sold an investment for over what you paid upon purchase. If your losses are above $3,000, you can carry them over to the next year and net them against your gains. This can sound pretty technical but your tax advisor or accountant should be knowledgeable about these rules.

HOW CAN YOU KNOW FOR SURE THAT IT'S TIME TO LET GO?

If you're having a hard time deciding whether to sell a stock, don't despair. View this as an opportunity to learn how to become more deliberative. Good decision making is a skill that's transferable to every area of life. Here's how to learn to make good investment decisions.

BALANCE RATIONAL DATA WITH INTUITION

First collect data that will help you look rationally at the stock you might sell by answering the following questions.

1. Is the stock performing well?
2. If it *is* performing well, does it represent too much of my portfolio?
3. If it's underperforming, do I see any prospects for improvement?
4. If I want to sell it because I need the cash to make a different investment, have I considered the tax consequences, and does the new opportunity provide the greatest potential?
5. Does the stock no longer meet my goals (for example, the growth rate is too low, the P/E ratio is too high, and so on)?
6. Has the company had a change in management or corporate philosophy that I don't agree with? (A corporate philosophy reflects the core values and beliefs; a chain of stores, for instance, that operates on the belief that shoppers will pay more for high-quality, healthy food.)
7. If I need the cash for an immediate expense, might it prove to be more to my advantage to get the money from another asset?

PURSERCISE: PUT TOGETHER A PORTFOLIO

There are no right or wrong decisions in this Pursercise. Simply pretend that you have $10,000 and want to invest $1,000 each in ten of the companies listed below. Place the numbers 1 through 10 beside each of your selections, in no particular order. Please note that I am

Investors can give themselves a security blanket by limiting their potential downside risk with a stop-loss order, which does exactly what it implies: at a predetermined point, it can stop you from losing money. Let's say you purchased a stock at $25 and then it declines to $20 a share. Should you sell and take a loss now or do you want to limit your losses at a certain price? You can place a stop-loss order at, say $15, which would convert to a market order if the shares fall that low. This is a particularly good stock trading strategy if you also place the trade as a GTC or "good till cancelled" order so you don't have to watch the stock every day.

not recommending that you buy or not buy stock in these companies. They were chosen purely at random. After you've made your decisions, you can discover how much you might have earned with these investments if you bought them in 1998 and allowed them to grow for ten years. Please don't peek at the answers in advance. The idea is to make your decisions as a reflection of your intuition and circle of competency.

___ A. Aetna: healthcare, dental, and pharmacy coverage
___ B. Altria: owns Philip Morris USA, the world's largest tobacco company
___ C. Amgen: biotechnology, maker of an osteoporosis drug
___ D. Avon: maker of skin care, makeup, bath and beauty products

___ E. Best Buy: electronics and appliance retailer

___ F. Cash America: owner of a chain of pawnshops

___ G. Clorox: major maker of cleaning products

___ H. Costco: membership-only warehouse shopping

___ I. Dior: makes and sells exclusive products, including handbags

___ J. Disney: owns theme parks and TV networks and produces films

___ K. eBay: An e-commerce auction website

___ L. Green Mountain: a provider of cleaner energy solutions

___ M. Gymboree: operates stores and play programs for infants up to age five

___ N. Johnson & Johnson: manufactures baby care, skin care, oral care, wound care, and women's health care products

___ O. Jones Apparel Group: designer, marketer, and wholesaler of apparel, footwear, and accessories

___ P. Kohls: department store chain selling discount clothing and goods

___ Q. LVMH: maker of among other things Louis Vuitton purses and Dom Perignon Champagne

___ R. McDonalds: fast food, famous for Big Macs

___ S. Medivation: makes Alzheimer's drug for those suffering mild and moderate symptoms

___ T. Northrop Grumman: provides systems and products in aerospace, ship building, etc., selling a variety of food and beverage products

___ U. Phillips Van Heusen: owners of the Calvin Klein, Arrow, Izod, and Kenneth Cole brands

___ V. Target: upscale discounter of trendy merchandise

___ W. Tiffany: worldwide exclusive jewelry company

___ X. United Healthcare: provides health care

___ Y. Varian: a maker of radiation therapy and X-ray imaging equipment

___ Z. Wynn Resorts: owners of a gambling empire

Once you've made selections, find them on the list below, fill in the tickers,* jot the earnings figure beside the company and add the total. You will find a space after the list to record the total on your selections.

A. Aetna (AET) $5,148

B. Altria (MO) $2,043

C. Amgen (AMGN) $3,690

D. Avon (AVP) $2,321

E. Best Buy (BBY) $6,632

F. Cash America (CSH) $2,916

G. Clorox (CLX) $1,150

H. Costco (COST) $2345

I. Dior (CHDRF) $445

J. Disney (DIS) $983

K. eBay (EBAY) $25,030

L. Green Mountain (GMCR) $51,549

M. Gymboree (GYMB) $3,910

N. Johnson & Johnson (JNJ) $4,139

---

* The three- or four-letter capped abbreviations following some company names are called "tickers," symbols that identify publicly traded shares of corporations. Tickers are named for the sound made by the old electronic machines that relayed stock information.

O. Jones Apparel Group (JNY), $806

P. Kohls (KSS) $1,798

Q. LVMH (LVMHF) $380

R. McDonalds (MCD) $1,938

S. Medivation (MDVN) $5,710

T. Northrop Grumman (NOC) $890

U. Phillips Van Heusen (PVH) $2,994

V. Target (TGT) $2,258

W. Tiffany (TIF) $2,258

X. United Healthcare (UNH) $7,149

Y. Varian (VAR) $11,652

Z. Wynn Resorts (WYNN) $1,256

Total your 10 stock selections:

1. (   ) $ _____

2. (   ) $ _____

3. (   ) $ _____

4. (   ) $ _____

5. (   ) $ _____

6. (   ) $ _____

7. (   ) $ _____

8. (   ) $ _____

9. (   ) $ _____

10. (   ) $ _____

Total: $ _____

(minus capital)   −$10,000

Profit: $ _____

So how did you do? Whatever your total, it can be put into perspective if you realize that if you'd deposited $10,00 into a savings account in 1998 at about 2 percent interest, a decade later you would have approximately $12,000, and minus your $10,000 principal, you would have earned $2,000. How does that compare with your fictional investment profit?

Finally, if you want to experience what it feels like to place a trade electronically without risking real money, there are several websites that have a virtual trading platform. Visit www.stockmarketgame .org, the website of The Stock Market Game, which teaches schools how to invest. You can join as an individual and begin managing a $100,000 portfolio.

Striking a Balance

Helen Greiner's story exemplifies the female/male strengths of persuasiveness and competitiveness. If the spirit moves you, write about how you envision utilizing these or similar traits to create a wealthy life.

You may want to use some of the following questions as guidelines:

- Who are some of the powerful speakers who have motivated me?
- Do I need to improve upon my own communication skills?
- What experiences have helped me enjoy the spirit of competition?
- How do I feel when I think someone is about to beat me at something?

_____

_____

_____

_____

_____

_____

_____

_____

_____

_____

FIVE | THE CLOSER I GET TO MY GOALS, THE BETTER BONDS MAKE ME FEEL

WEALTHY HABIT # 5: FOCUS

CLEO, ONE OF MY BUDDIES, TALKS NONSTOP ABOUT hoping to meet Mr. Right, and maybe she will someday. She's an attractive attorney with a good sense of humor, and she sure knows how to make great investment choices. I can't say the same about her romantic choices. Cleo always finds something she doesn't like about each new guy.

One time when I challenged her about being too picky, she said that just because I was going home with a prince every night didn't mean she had to settle for a frog. That got me laughing, but judging from a few of the men she's brought around, some of these guys *are* princes in disguise. She doesn't agree and continues to complain that one guy is too short or another is too heavy.

Somewhere out there, I told her, a woman is kicking herself because decades ago, she was foolish enough to say the same thing about Warren Buffett. Later, when I challenged her to explain what she didn't like about one guy, she started sounding vague. "He was nice, but I just wasn't feeling him." She meant that he was boring.

Like the Colin Firth character in the film *Bridget Jones's Diary,* bonds are not all *that* exciting. In the long run, however, you'd be wise to consider Mr. Sure-and-Steady. Unlike the guy who broke your heart, bonds will be there for you.

Bonds, the quiet sidekicks of stocks, send out streams of interest income while stocks spurt and tank their way up and down the charts. By holding steady when stocks zig and zag, bonds can stabilize your portfolio. Bonds are not immune to events in the global markets, but a strong commitment to these investment instruments can put you in an enviable position when stocks decline.

The notion that bonds are lacking in allure is reflected in the media. If you turn to the financial news pages and scan headings for "bonds," you may find only a few columns devoted to the subject. Meanwhile, you'll probably see pages of stock and mutual fund listings, plus other stock-related categories. Bonds, if they are listed at all, don't get equal billing. This chapter is written to convince you that you should keep your heart . . . er, I mean purse open to the possibility that there might be some bonding in your future.

In looking for an analogous romantic model to describe how bonds can encourage a Wealthy Focus, consider how slim your chances of creating happiness would be if you were in an angry, nerve-wracking relationship. How can you make headway in achieving your goals if you've been sitting up all night worrying about whether he'll show up before dawn or if he really is out with the guys? Now consider the alternative: You've got someone who understands what you want and he provides steady support as you move forward. In this manner, bonds can help you develop a Wealthy Focus.

WEALTHY HABIT # 5: A WEALTHY FOCUS

· ·

A Wealthy Focus helps you set priorities and eliminate distractions as you pursue your goals. Stating specific desired outcomes allows you to stay on course in the face of adversity.

· ·

UNDERSTANDING BONDS

Take note, Purse Ladies: Just as it takes a little more work to see the prince inside the soul of the nice guy, it takes a little more effort to understand bonds. But isn't it good to know that once you commit, you'll have someone or something that you can count on?

Bonds are the new sexy. They're sold by corporations and by federal, state, and local governments and similar entities for the purpose of raising money and with the promise that the principal and interest will be repaid on a specific date. Think of bonds as micro loans. As a bond purchaser, you're the one who is making the loan. Here's how bonds work: The borrowers (corporations or governments) make regular payments (interest) and promise to repay you the amount of the original loan (principal) when the bond becomes due at a future date (when they mature).

Most bonds are issued at something that's called "face" or "par value" in denominations of $1,000. The issuing organization offers the bonds for sale for the purpose of raising capital for expansion or to refinance existing debt. Similar to what happens behind the scenes with an initial public stock offering, a syndicate or group of firms sells the bonds to institutions or to brokerages that will make the bonds available to investors.

Bonds offer a set interest rate and a maturity date. Because of the set interest rate, bonds are often called "fixed-income securities." You'll know what you'll be getting and when to expect it. This is good for the budget, especially if you are no longer working and need a fixed stream of dependable income.

Government bonds are considered safest because of the government's ability to tax citizens to repay its debts. Corporate bonds are riskier, but less so than stocks. That's because when a corporation repays investors, bondholders get paid first, while stockholders are second in line. From 1926 through 2007, long-term bonds have generated an average return of 5.4 percent versus 10.4 percent for stocks.

Yes, the overall return from bonds is typically lower than with stocks. But as in love relationships, you have to be willing to accept trade-offs. For instance, when Cleo told me that she was unhappy with her newest guy because he "never talks," I pointed out that this also meant he wouldn't be likely to argue, either. The trade-off with bonds is that in exchange for the security of getting your principal returned at a future date, you forgo future growth potential or the higher returns associated with stocks.

WHAT BONDS PROVIDE: INCOME AND SAFETY

With bonds, most of the return comes from *income*. Simply put, if you need current income or less volatility, you invest in bonds. With bonds you are paid interest every six months. This interest income is the "current return" or "yield."

Bonds offer *safety of principal* and are considered conservative investments, typically more secure than stocks. If the investor holds the bond until maturity, she receives principal or her original investment. In the event of bankruptcy, all creditors and bondholders are paid in full before stockholders receive any return of their investment. Just as there are degrees of risk in stocks, this is also the case with bonds.

A Purseonality Profile: Cathy Hughes

A Woman with a Wealthy Focus

Cathy Hughes knows how to eliminate obstacles that might distract her from her goals. This owner of the media giant Radio One built a company that went public in 1999, when the shares of her company were issued and traded on the stock market. Hughes became the first black woman to head a public company.

Hughes built her $2 billion enterprise by sheer force of will, creativity, and shining intelligence. I should know. She gave me my first radio job. I was a vice president at Fidelity Investments in 1995, when Eric St. James interviewed me for Radio One; he later suggested that I needed to host a show teaching people how to invest. A year later I wrote Cathy Hughes with my idea for a show called "Moneyworks." Imagine my surprise when she invited me to come in for a discussion, and then began training me to host a show.

It didn't take me long to understand how Cathy Hughes had become the most powerful woman in radio. This is a woman who knows how to focus on realizing her dreams. In 1973, some people must have thought that the Omaha, Nebraska, divorcée and single mom was taking on a losing proposition when she accepted the job of sales manager at Howard University's WHUR radio, which was thirty-eighth in its market and struggling on $250,000 a year in ad revenue. Under Hughes' masterful leadership revenues rose to $3 million and the station moved up to number three in its market. During this period, Hughes created what fans of soulful slow jazz and R&B would recognize as the Quiet Storm, a radio format that has been copied by hundreds of stations.

Hungry for the next challenge, Hughes turned her sights to a station that had been off the air for more than a decade, WYCB, in the District of Columbia, and turned it into the country's first twenty-four-hour gospel station. With these successes under her belt, Hughes was ready to become an owner. She weathered thirty-two bank rejections, and then, in 1980, two African-American venture capitalists and a woman bank loan officer lent her enough so that she was able to raise the $1.5 million needed to buy and run DC's troubled WOL-AM.

According to *Ebony*, which chronicled Hughes' story, the former owner had fired all the employees, and in retaliation, many of them had destroyed or carted away what they could—including the music. Hughes went home, grabbed her record collection, and kept the station on the air. But her problems had only just begun. With interest rates as high as 28 percent compounding on her loans, her house went into foreclosure and her car was repossessed. She saved the day by selling the family heirloom, her great-grandmother's pocket watch, which had been made by slaves, for $50,000.

Hughes then moved into the station, slept in a sleeping bag, cooked on a hot plate, and bathed in the station's public bathroom. She defied prevailing wisdom by transforming her R&B station into a twenty-four-hour talk format, and took to the airwaves, hosting her own talk show. During her fourteen-year-run, she became known as "the voice of the community," turned a profit, and started building an empire, station by station. By 1999, she owned twenty-nine stations, nine of them in the top twenty African-American markets, and had amassed a personal fortune of $300 million. She raised $172 million when she took her company public in an initial public offering (IPO).

Purseonality Assessment

Hughes's story can remind you to:

Be Decisive. Like Hughes, you may be forced to make difficult decisions, and life won't necessarily give you much time. I'm not suggesting acting rashly; sometimes the best thing to do is nothing at all.

Remain Flexible. When Hughes couldn't afford to hire another employee, she hosted her own show. Whether you work for yourself or someone else, develop your skills beyond your expertise. This will open the way for more opportunities than you'd ever imagined.

Put Together a Game Plan. Hughes knew that she wanted to build a radio empire and set about doing it. People who plan are far more likely to succeed than those who just drift and let life happen to them. Game plans aren't written in stone; they can be altered.

WHY BONDS ARE ESSENTIAL TO YOUR PORTFOLIO

Delores, 37, a social worker, didn't start out in life focusing on the future. In fact, she says that when she was attending college, she lived for the minute and never even had a thought about where her next dollar would come from. Raised in a wealthy Southern family, Delores says that fifteen years ago she was spending more than $500 a week, using the credit cards and generous allowance her parents provided to her as a student. "I loved surfing and spring breaks, until I realized that millions of poor people were suffering," Delores says. She underwent a religious conversion and dedicated her life to working with young women from impoverished families. She has since won kudos for her work with girl gangs in the northeastern neighborhoods of Brooklyn, New York, an area that accounted for nearly half of the borough's murders in 2008.

Enraged by her career choice, her father cut Delores off financially. He told her to either fend for herself or accept her family's way of life—which she describes as full of gas-guzzling cars, nonstop shopping, and women who don't even consider careers. Delores chose to go it alone and never looked back. During her first five years on her own, she kept her expenses low by tolerating "lousy" roommates and scraping together money to rent space at a farmer's market, where she sold pecan tarts, and she saved $30,000.

Because Delores had seen so many of her young charges carrying Apple iPods, she invested in the company. If you'd invested $28,000 in Apple a decade ago, you'd have made a profit of $300,000. Delores invested $9,000 in Apple, and in five years the stock was valued at $100,000. Fearful of losing what she'd had, she decided to diversify and invested half of her profits in corporate and government bonds.

Delores called her broker and explained that she wanted to protect some of the profits she had earned and that she might need her money to make a deposit on an apartment. He suggested high-grade, short-term corporate and municipal bonds. Delores invested $25,000 in New York Metropolitan Transit Municipal bonds and the other $25,000 in Pfizer Pharmaceutical bonds. Her broker estimated that this bond investment would pay her $2,250 annually for the next five years, an additional $11,250. This didn't sound very attractive at the time compared to the outsized profits she had made off her Apple stock.

Looking back, Delores was delighted at having sold her Apple stock at the height of the market in January 2007. The Apple shares that remain in her portfolio are worth a lot less now. Delores knew she wouldn't earn the high returns she'd enjoyed with stocks, but she was looking for a safer haven. She understands that the economic downturn that began in 2007 is no anomaly, and that bonds can help her survive a bear market.

HOW DELORES FILLED HER PURSE WITH BONDS

Delores's stock broker placed an order for the bonds. Remember, both stocks and bonds are traded or purchased through an exchange. Bonds are traded on the over-the-counter exchange, and this is how a bond, like the one Delores chose, would be listed.

Pfizer Pharmaceutical 5%, 1/2012 bond

This describes a bond that would pay Delores interest at the "coupon rate" of 5 percent and mature in January 2012. Delores purchased twenty-five bonds at $1,000 each, investing $25,000, and received a payment of $625 every six months.

She also purchased New York Metropolitan Transit Authority Municipal Bonds 4%, 1/2012, paying 4 percent interest and maturing in January 2012. She was paid $500 every six months. Delores's $50,000 investment kicked out a total of $2250 annually, a grand total of $11,250 when the bonds matured. This was thousands more than she could have earned in a money market.

She also had the comfort of knowing that her original investment would be returned to her in 2012. What would happen if Delores wanted to sell one of her bonds and interest rates had declined and now similar bonds yielded 4 percent? Delores could sell her 5 percent bonds at a premium, or for $1,250 per bond. (See table on p. 106.)

This would reflect the fact that her bond's interest rate or coupon is paying 5 percent and therefore more valuable than those issued at the current lower rate. The coupon rate always stays the same but the bond's price will move up and down. It's very much like a see-saw. If interest rates go up, the bond's price goes down. If interest rates go down, the bond's price goes up. Let's work through this example:

Pfizer Pharmaceutical 5%, 1/2012

- Purchase price: $1,000
- Coupon rate: 5 percent = $50 annually
- Current yield: 5 percent
- Maturity date: January 1, 2012

The second column in the table below shows how a 5 percent yield is calculated in the example above, the next column shows what happens if interest rates decline to 4 percent, and the last column shows how bonds react when interest rates are increased to 6 percent.

IMPACT OF INTEREST RATES ON BOND PRICES			
Current Interest Rate	5%	4%	6%
Face Value	$1,000	$1,000	$1,000
Coupon	5%	5%	5%
Current Value	$1,000	$1250	$833
Income/Price=	$50/$1,000=	$50/$1,250=	$50/$833=
Current Yield	5%	4%	6%

HOW INFLATION AFFECTS BOND PRICES

Another risk Delores took when she chose the security of bonds over stocks was the risk of bond prices declining in response to rises in inflation. This happens when the Federal Reserve, the nation's central bank, which guides U.S. monetary policy, increases interest rates to protect the economy from inflation. As a bond investor Delores watched her bonds fluctuate in value, but she was not concerned because she continued to receive the interest payments and had the comfort of knowing that her original investment would be returned when the bonds matured. And one of the advantages Delores got by being paid twice a year is that she could reinvest the income sooner.

THE IMPORTANCE OF BOND RATINGS

Of course, safety of principal depends on the issuer's credit strength. Bondholders have learned that although they can have a reasonable expectation that the principal (the face amount of the bond) will be paid back in full on the maturity date, that is not guaranteed. In addition, if they sell their bonds before maturity, they take their chances that the current price of the bond may be more or less than what they paid.

Just as a bank chooses whom to lend to on the basis of credit history, you can choose which bonds to purchase based on credit rating. The most frequently used ratings sources are Moody's, Standard & Poors and A.M. Best. Their ratings are broken down into six basic categories on page 108.

Corporations benefit from having a high credit rating. One way for corporations to gain the highest credit rating is to purchase insurance from a monoline insurer (a type of insurer that provides services to one industry) such as AMBAC (American Bond Assurance Corporation) or MBIA. These companies provide insurance that guarantees that you will receive your principal and interest in the event the company defaults. This is why Delores's broker suggested that she purchase bonds with a AAA rating even though she would earn a lower

BOND RATING CHART			
	Standard & Poors	Moody's	A.M. Best
Prime Investment grade	AAA	Aaa	aaa
High grade Investment grade	AA	A	aa
Medium Investment grade	A	A	a
Lower Investment grade	BBB	Baa	bbb
High-yield or junk	BB	Ba	bb, b
High-yield or junk	B, CCC, CC	B, Caa	ccc, cc, c

return. While Delores chose to buy a AAA rated bond, you may want to purchase bonds with a lower rating and earn a higher return. But be advised if the issuer defaults, you will put your investment at risk.

THE LANGUAGE OF BONDS

Delores worked with a broker, but because she knew that the biggest risk to her investment was her own ignorance, she learned the language of bonds. Should you choose to invest in bonds, you will want to understand the four key terms that follow.

Callable bond: Bonds sold with the stipulation that the company can "call" (or redeem them) before maturity, meaning there's a chance that the bond will be paid off before maturity. To offset this feature, callable bonds typically pay a slightly higher interest rate.

Convertible bonds: These allow investors to convert the value of their bonds into shares in the company, if and when it becomes advantageous. Convertible bonds typically pay a slightly lower rate of interest than nonconvertible bonds.

Default risk: There's always a possibility that the company might not be able to pay you back. This is why it's important to pay attention to an issuer's credit rating. In exchange for increased risk of default, a company or issuer will increase the interest it pays to make its bond more attractive and to make up for its higher risk.

High-yield or junk bonds: These pay higher interest rates to make up for the company's poorer credit rating. With bonds rated BB, Ba, B, or B- there is concern that the company will not have the ability to make timely interest payments, or may default and not return investors' principal—so buyer beware.

COZYING UP TO GOVERNMENT BONDS

When you think of government bonds, the first thing that comes to mind may be a savings bond. They are the most widely held security. Savings bonds include Series EE, Series HH, and Series I bonds that are sold in denominations as little as $25. These can be purchased at any local bank.

When I became a stockbroker, clients often asked me to research the current value of their savings bonds in order to determine whether or not the bonds had matured and were still earning interest. In many cases, the person inquiring had inherited the bonds and had no clue as to their value. Today people can simply go online to www.savingsbonds .gov to get more information on bonds and current interest rates.

Americans consider savings bonds the safest of investments because of their faith in the U.S. government. Shelly, a caller to my radio show, was introduced to bonds as a teenager. "I started investing in savings bonds when I was seventeen. The bonds were mailed to my mother's house. It was an easy way for me to put money aside, and I forgot that I had them." Years later, Shelly was in the process of buying a house and feeling pummeled by all the unanticipated expenses that kept cropping up, when her mother sent over a box filled with her birth certificate, report cards, and other paperwork. Going through the documents, Shelly found she had accumulated close to $10,000 in U.S. savings bonds. She says, "I didn't spend it all, I just used what I needed on my down payment—but it sure was a nice gift to myself."

Savings bonds are no longer issued in paper form but you can easily invest in savings bonds electronically from your bank account. First, you go to www.savingsbonds.gov and open an online account. Second, you supply your bank information. Third, you choose the type you want to buy. Fourth, you choose the amount you want. Your saving bonds will be held at the United States Treasury. Be sure to remember to save your account number. You will be able to check your account value twenty-four hours a day, seven days a week.

"OTHER" GOVERNMENT BONDS

In addition to savings bonds, the federal government sells treasury securities to raise money to operate the government. Treasury securities include bills, notes, and bonds. Treasury bills are short-term securities that are issued with maturities of less than one year, whereas treasury notes are issued with maturities of two, three, five, and seven years. Treasury bonds are issued with maturities of thirty years. As of April 2008, the minimum price for buying treasuries was lowered from $1,000 to $100. Many investors complain about the low interest rates they receive on treasuries. However, if you are a conservative investor, these are the safest investment because of the U.S. government's financial standing even in an economic down-turn.

HOW TO PURCHASE BONDS

If you are interested in purchasing U.S. government bonds, you can go through a broker (which might be the simplest way to handle the transaction) or you can purchase them direct. If you choose to buy them direct, first visit www.treasurydirect.gov and view the auction schedule. Second, establish an online account. Third, have funds transferred electronically from your bank account. Fourth, choose which bills, bonds, or notes you want to purchase. Once purchased, the securities will be held in your account with the United States Treasury. Be sure to remember to save your account number. You will be able to check your account value twenty-four hours a day, seven days a week.

INCOME, NO STRINGS (TAXES) ATTACHED

Delores loves municipal bonds, or as they are fondly called, "munis," because they offer tax-free income and are issued by state and local governments. States and cities rarely default on their debts, and these bonds certainly are safer than those issued by corporations. In terms of safety, munis are only slightly behind federal bonds.

Delores also loves munis because as her income from her pastry business increased, her tax bracket increased. Munis are popular with investors who are in higher tax brackets. The higher your income, the more taxes you pay and appealing tax-free income is. To compute your tax equivalent yield use the formula provided.

> Here is a simple formula for calculating whether you need munis for tax advantages: Subtract your tax bracket from 1.00 and divide the tax-free interest rate by the difference. Here is an example of an investor in a 33 percent tax bracket who is considering purchasing a municipal bond that is yielding 3.5 percent. Subtract the tax bracket from the number 1.00 (1.00 − .33 =.67) and then divide the yield by the difference, or 3.5 percent ÷ .67, and the result is a tax equivalent yield of 5.22 percent.

Delores is also enthusiastic about buying zero-coupon municipal bonds, especially those rated AAA. Zero-coupon bonds work like savings bonds in that they are issued at a discount and mature at their face value years later. This way, in the small chance that the city defaults, she would still get paid. She's willing to accept a slightly lower interest rate to make certain that her bonds are completely safe.

Many investors purchase government bonds for their tax advantages. Federal and state governments engage in a reciprocal deal—the

ZERO-COUPON BONDS

They don't offer interest payments, are sold at a discount, and mature at face value. However, the interest accrues and is taxed annually, which is why these types of bonds are more favorable when purchased for tax-deferred individual retirement accounts or in the form of a tax-free municipal bond.

federal government promises not to tax state bond income, and the state governments promise not to tax federal bond income. Municipal bonds that are purchased by residents of the state are generally exempt from both federal and state income tax. Here are a few other terms that will help you understand the types of municipal bonds.

General obligation munis: Used for the construction and operation of highways and water and sewage systems. Investors are paid from a general tax fund.

Revenue munis: Investors are paid from the revenues earned from the funded project, for example baseball stadiums and/or convention centers.

High-yield munis: They fund specific revenue-generating projects, such as hospitals and airports. Because they are also considered a higher risk than more general obligation munis, they also offer a higher interest rate.

BONDS ARE THERE WHEN
YOU NEED THEM

By 2009, interest rates had declined, and Delores's bonds had appreciated, and the overall return on some of her bonds allowed her to put $50,000 down on her own apartment. "My place is tiny, but I don't have to share it with weird roommates. I shut the door and feel a little jolt of pleasure."

Shortly after she bought her place, her father came calling. When she told him she had hired two part-time employees, and explained her bond investments, "Daddy actually said that I reminded him of the son he never had. It didn't occur to him to think of me as a woman with a good head on her shoulders. But that's my daddy for you."

His admiration for his daughter didn't change his mind about wanting to control her life. "He offered to put up cash if I moved home. He said that he would donate to a program for teenage girls and that I could run it. I explained that my clients need me to be here in New York. I'm teaching the girls I work with about money. A lot of them are tough . . . on the outside anyway, but they think men are supposed to be the big dogs. I tell 'em if they've got money of their own they can do the barkin'. See, I'm barkin' at my daddy. If I'd taken his money, it would have still been his."

Delores has another reason for wanting to stay put. She's fallen in love with an organic farmer whose stall is near hers at the farmers' market where she operates her outdoor bakery stall. The two plan to marry. Delores laughs at her situation. She left the South hoping she would run into some "city guy," but she wound up falling for someone who is just the opposite. It sounds like a guy-next-door type turned out to be Delores's Prince Charming. I hope Cleo is taking note.

THE CLOSER YOU GET TO YOUR GOALS, THE BETTER YOU'LL FEEL ABOUT BONDS

If you're ten years or more from your goal: If you're in your twenties or early thirties and saving for retirement, bonds should make up less than 10 percent of your portfolio.

If you're six to nine years from your goal: An advisor may recommend that you continue to keep most of your assets in stocks, but you might also be advised to allocate about 30 percent of your portfolio to bonds, due to the erratic behavior of the market.

If you're three to five years from your goal: Delores, for instance, was saving to buy property in New York City and she figured that she was about four years from needing her money. Bonds offered her psychological comfort. If you have a time horizon of three to five years until you will need access to your funds, a financial advisor may recommend that you invest more than 50 percent of your investment in bonds because you know that your principal will be returned and available.

If you're retiring soon: As you move closer to retirement, you will probably want to move more of your assets to bonds so that you can reliably generate the income stream you need. Think of all the investors who lost half or even more of their retirement savings in the bear market that began in 2007. Many of these investors would have had a different outcome had they diversified their portfolios with a heavy mix of bonds.

DECIDING HOW BONDS FIT IN TO YOUR PORTFOLIO

What about you? What dreams are you focusing on that might be helped by bond investments? You don't want your dreams to go awry because of an economic downturn that might cause stock prices to fall just when you are planning to cash in. Here is a quick exercise you can use to determine how much of your portfolio should be divided between stocks and bonds:

PURSERCISE: PURSE ALLOCATOR

What percentage of bonds should you have in your purse?

TIME FRAME

1. I plan to start withdrawing money from my investments in

Less than five years	2 points
Five to ten years	6 points
Eleven years or more	10 points

SCORE _____

2. Once I begin withdrawing funds from my investments, I plan to use them over the next

Five to ten years	2 points
Ten to twenty years	6 points
Thirty or more	10 points

SCORE _____

CURRENT SITUATION

3. My investment knowledge and experience could be described as

No experience   2 points
Some experience but I feel uncomfortable making decisions on
my own   6 points
Experienced, I have some investments but need assistance
occasionally   8 points
Very experienced, I make my own financial
decisions   10 points
SCORE _____

4. My current portfolio consists of

(only one choice; assume you own some or all of prior investments)
Bank savings accounts and money market funds   2 points
Treasury bonds, CDs, or bond mutual funds   6 points
Stocks and/or stock mutual funds   8 points
International stocks and international funds   10 points
SCORE _____

RISK TOLERANCE

5. Which one of the following statements best describes your feelings
toward risk?

I make investments that have a low degree of risk   2 points
I take a balanced approach and invest equally in high
and low risk   4 points
I want to be aggressive and lean more toward high risk with
some in lower risk   6 points

I want the potential for the greatest return and only
invest in higher risk   8 points
SCORE _____

6. If the stock market dropped 20 percent and your investments
followed suit, what would you do?

Liquidate all of it and transfer to a money market   2 points
Sell half of it and leave the rest   4 points
I would leave it alone   6 points
I would buy more   8 points
SCORE _____

Now add up all of your points from questions 1 through 6.

TOTAL SCORE _____

Find out where you fall in the legend below.

Aggressive Growth Portfolio   50 or more
Growth Portfolio   40 to 49
Balanced Portfolio   30 to 39
Conservative Portfolio   20 to 29

Now look at the following portfolios and identify which might best
suit your situation based on your total score.

	STOCKS	BONDS	CASH
Short-Term Portfolio			100%
Conservative Portfolio	50%	30%	20%
Balanced Portfolio	50%	40%	10%
Growth Portfolio	70%	25%	5%
Aggressive Growth Portfolio	85%	15%	0%

Striking a Balance

In this chapter, Cathy Hughes demonstrated the female/male strengths of spontaneity and determination. If the spirit moves you, write about how you envision utilizing these or similar traits to create a wealthy life.

You may want to use some of the following questions as guidelines:

- What experiences taught me the value of being spontaneous?
- What are the areas in which I have proved to be inflexible and that I hope to change?
- How do I need to demonstrate greater determination in creating a wealthy life?
- Who is the most determined person that I know of whom I'd like to use as my role model?

_____

_____

_____

_____

_____

_____

_____

_____

_____

SIX | A POOLING OF THE PURSES: PURCHASING MUTUAL FUNDS

WEALTHY HABIT #6:
CREATING A WEALTHY SYSTEM

THE EXPRESSION "TWO HEADS ARE BETTER THAN ONE" reminds us that when people work together, they generate powerful results. It's the same when it comes to bringing purses together to generate wealth. The word "mutual" refers to something shared by two or more people, and mutual fund investors are empowered by the feminine spirit of collaboration.

In addition to buying stocks individually, investors can purchase them in packages known as "mutual funds" that offer stocks in a variety of companies. Here's how they work. Mutual fund investors contribute to a massive pool of money that is managed by financial professionals who invest in stocks and bonds on their behalf. Because the pool of money is so much larger than what the average individual investor generally has when working solo, mutual fund shareholders are purchasing clout in the marketplace.

Up to this point I've focused on offering you foundational knowledge about stocks and bonds. I introduced those investment vehicles first because, as the saying goes, you had to have been there. It's difficult to understand mutual funds if you don't know how individual investing works. To that end, you've seen that when it comes to buying specific companies, individual stock purchases offer a sense of control. But keeping your holdings diversified requires a lot of attention.

This chapter is written to help you understand why I almost always steered new investors who had less than $100,000 toward mutual funds. These investment vehicles seem tailor-made for the multitasking modern woman who understands that she needs to put her purse to work but who doesn't have the time to focus on her portfolio. And mutual funds tend to be affordable. For about a $1,000 you can hire an Ivy League–educated money manager along with a roster of analysts whose sole purpose is to meet your financial objectives. It's like playing the field and having several suitors at your beck and call. Now ladies, what could be wrong with that?

Let me answer that question, because mutual funds do have some disadvantages. Yes, they do require a lot less of an investor's attention, but that also means relinquishing control, since you don't have a say in what investments the fund makes. Mutual funds are considered less risky than purchasing individual stocks, but that also means they generally (but not always) yield lower returns. Funds also charge management and carrying fees that cut into profits and capital. And there's always the chance that your mutual fund manager can have a bad year and not select investments that yield good returns.

Despite these drawbacks, mutual funds remain hugely popular. By 2008, ninety-six million people had put $11 trillion into funds. Because these funds are invested in a variety of stocks and bonds, they level the playing field for novice investors by offering diversification, which is important because it reduces volatility—the up and down movement of the market. Fund managers also reduce volatility in mutual funds by investing in different companies and industries that are less likely to be adversely impacted at the same time. (But if you do have a particular area of interest, you can find mutual funds that specialize in "sectors" or specific industries, such as retail, energy, real estate, technology, health, and financials.)

The economic downturn that began in 2007 impacted all industries, but shares increased in companies such as Walmart and Auto-Zone as consumers cut back on spending. Mutual fund managers look to invest in companies that will profit in good and bad times. So while some of the investments in your fund may go down, others might remain high, offsetting losses.

Another advantage of mutual funds is that they make it easy for you to invest small sums of money periodically and systematically through payroll or checking account deductions. This method can turbo charge your savings. Buying mutual funds regularly allows you to "dollar cost average," which means you invest a specific amount on a set schedule, regardless of what the market is doing. So dollar cost averaging enables you to buy shares automatically when the price is lower and then buy fewer shares when the price is higher. By purchasing shares systematically, you reduce your chances of buying shares at their highest levels. It averages out your cost per share. This enhances your ability to adopt the habit of maintaining a Wealthy Focus.

One of my colleagues in Baltimore, Dr. Katherine Collier, is a dentist and a big mutual fund investor. She cautions novices to mutual funds to expect "ups and downs," just as you would with any investment. At the same time, she points out that she has experienced an extraordinarily high level of success in mutual funds.

A mother of two young adults, she lost her husband, a psychiatrist, in 1994 when he died of an aortic aneurysm. Shortly afterward she received a lump sum on her husband's insurance policy, and she decided to put some of that in mutual funds. "I knew nothing about investing, so I had to teach myself."

She spent weeks researching various investment opportunities before putting $20,000 each into five mutual funds. "I invested just before the bull market of the late 1990s. After a couple of years, when my balances doubled, I thought, 'There is no way I could pull that many teeth or finish that many crowns to earn this kind of money.' Dentistry is hard work; it's high stress. My funds hadn't required much work, just making phone calls. It was like going into a casino and hitting the jackpots. I realized that it just made common sense to invest."

She held on to her funds for more than a decade. "The balance of one went up to $100,000. On the average, I quadrupled my money." She has also endured times when her funds lost value. In the long run, though, Dr. Collier earned thousands of dollars more than she invested, enough to help her buy a home and pay school tuition for her two daughters.

If they gave out prizes for these kinds of achievements, Dr. Collier would win high honors in the Order of the Purse Realm. In a matter of years she recovered from her husband's unexpected death, continued working in her practice, and raised two daughters, while increasing the size of her purse. On the home front she was able to pull off these feats by setting up a network of family, friends, and associates. When it came to her finances, she hired a team of world-class money managers who offered a diverse portfolio and financial liquidity. You, too, can hire your own dream team for about $1,000, which is the approximate cost of buying into the average mutual fund, and let the money managers do most of the work for you. Professional money managers actually account for the bulk of trading volume in the financial markets. They influence the movement of stock prices and ultimately the fortunes of millions of investors.

It's always important to remind you that as with any investments, mutual funds involve risks. It bears repeating that in the marketplace, as the level of risk increases so does the potential for greater profits. Investors take risks because they want to make their money grow. That also means losing money, but they believe their bottom lines will be richer in the long run. During the economic downturn that began in 2007, a number of mutual funds shed money. Many savvy investors who could afford to hold on did just that, continuing to invest regularly, with an eye on the future. I met many women who felt they had put a good system in place, and they were committed to sticking with it.

WEALTHY HABIT # 6: A WEALTHY SYSTEM

• •

Creating a Wealthy System is all about assembling a safety net, which is what you get by investing in mutual funds. This is the most pragmatic of the 7 Wealthy Habits. When you set up a Wealthy System, it can help you bring aspects of your life together to operate as a whole and keep you moving forward financially.

• •

A MUTUAL FUND YOU CAN
SET AND FORGET

I've included instructions below for finding a mutual fund that suits your needs. But if you really want to simplify matters, consider an index mutual fund. Index funds were tailor made for do-it-yourselfers. An index fund tracks an index such as the Standard & Poors 500. These funds are literally put on automatic pilot as the stocks are identical to the index that they mirror, so when the index goes up, so does your fund, and vice versa.

These kinds of shares eliminate the risk of individual stocks, the risk of market sectors, and the risk of manager selection.

Just like that great pair of pumps that never go out style, index funds can be an essential portfolio basic in your Wealthy System. You should decide to do your homework, as Dr. Collier did, and find a fund that reflects your goals and objectives.

SELECT A MUTUAL FUND
IN SEVEN EASY STEPS

Step 1. Review Your Objectives

Understanding your objectives is the key to selecting a mutual fund that is right for you. It will be helpful to review and answer the following questions:

- What is your goal or objective for this investment? For instance, you might be accumulating an emergency fund, down payment on a home, college savings, or money for retirement or to help you become financially independent.

- How much time are you giving yourself to achieve this
  goal?
  - Short term is three to five years.
  - Intermediate is five to ten years.
  - Long term is ten years or more.
- How much risk can you afford and are you willing to take?
  Low, moderate, or high?

Dr. Collier's goals included educating her daughters and saving for retirement. Knowing she would need to pay college costs for
her daughters in several years and that she wanted to retire in ten to
fifteen years, she looked for funds that had a good track record for
growth. She felt certain that she had a high level of tolerance for risk.
She says she was not the sort of investor who bit her nails to the quick
when reading about market declines. Her objective was capital appreciation, or put more simply, she wanted to grow the proceeds from the
insurance policy so she could take care of herself and her daughters.
Growth, income, and capital preservation are some of the most common objectives of investors. Were you able to determine your objectives?

Step 2. Determine Which Mutual Funds
Match Your Objectives

Mutual funds or simply "funds" as they are called, come in different shapes and sizes. You can match your objective to the appropriate
type of fund.

For the purposes of our work, I've narrowed them into four categories.

TYPE OF FUND	OBJECTIVE	TIME FRAME	RISK LEVEL
Money Market	Liquidity	Short	Low
Bonds	Income & Capital Preservation	Intermediate	Moderate
Growth and Income	Capital Appreciation/ Income	Intermediate/ Long Term	Moderate
Aggressive Growth	Capital Appreciation	Long Term	High

Money market funds: When you want your money to remain liquid, and your objective is preservation of capital. These funds are similar to savings accounts but do not carry FDIC Insurance. They generally pay higher interest rates of 1 to 2 percent above bank savings and money market accounts. This type of fund is appropriate for short time frames and low risk tolerance.

Bond funds: When you want current income and your objective is to preserve capital. These types of funds work well for investors who have intermediate time frames of three or more years and low to moderate risk tolerance.

Growth and income funds: These work well for individuals seeking a split between growth and income. These funds invest in large companies whose stocks pay dividends. Therefore investors benefit through stock appreciation and through dividend income. These funds are for time frames of five years or more and moderate risk tolerance.

Growth funds: These are tailored for investors who want their money to grow over time and can keep their money invested while weathering economic cycles and the ups and downs of the market. These funds are for investors with time frames of seven years or more and high risk tolerance.

PURSERCISE:
MATCHING THE FUND TO YOUR NEEDS

Answer the following questions to determine the fund that best suits your needs. Choose one, and assign the appropriate point value.

1. What will you use the money for?

Emergency fund	2 points
Home	3 points
College savings	4 points
Retirement	5 points

2. How much time are you giving yourself to achieve this goal?

Immediately	2 points
Short term (three to five years)	3 points
Intermediate (five to ten years)	4 points
Long term (ten to twenty years)	5 points

3. How much risk can you afford and are you willing to take?

No risk	2 points
Low risk	3 points
Moderate risk	4 points
High risk	5 points
TOTAL _____	

Now find the type of fund that corresponds to your total points:

Money market	0–6 pts
Bonds	6–9 pts
Growth and income	10–12
Growth	12–14
Aggressive growth	15+

Does your fund choice fit your needs? Take a look at the following scenarios.

0–6 points: Money Market Fund

Yes, you've got the money in hand for that transmission that just went out in your car. Or if you've had it up to your neck with your frustrating boss, you'll have a few dollars in hand to tide you over until you get a new gig.

6–9 points: Bond Fund

You love your roommate, but year after year it seems your space is getting smaller. You're ready to strike out on your own. This fund will give you the well-needed funds for a down payment on your new digs.

Or the market dropped 20 percent and your stomach dropped with it. Time to move a few dollars into a safer place.

10–12 points: Growth and Income Fund

You're forty-five and you can't believe you are still paying off college loans. You're determined to have funds available for your ten-year-old so she's not mired in debt after college. Choose this fund to help build a reserve so you'll have enough by the time she's ready for school without risking too much.

12–14 points: Growth Fund

You just transferred jobs and you have a new benefit plan. Choose this fund to invest in your company's plan or a Roth IRA.

15+ points: Aggressive Growth Fund

Whoo hoo! Just out of college and the world is your oyster! You're determined to retire by forty-five. You can jump right into these aggressive funds and still have time to rebound if things don't work out as planned.

Step 3. Are You a Boutique girl or a One-Stop Shopper?

Consider whether you want a fund that specializes in a particular size or sector. Are you the type that might buy lingerie at Victoria's Secret, pop into Bath & Body Works for the latest aromatherapy fragrance, and then venture into M.A.C. for their newest blue eye shadow? Or would you rather step into Saks and find it all in one place? If you have the time to shop and customize your portfolio, then you can choose funds that focus on specific types of industries or on a specific size company. If your time is limited, then you're better off choosing a broad diversified fund. Both will meet your objective of growth, but with varying degrees of risk and time spent.

GROWTH FUNDS AT A GLANCE		
Type of Growth Funds	Type of Companies	Type of Risk
Aggressive Growth	Small cap and emerging companies	Very aggressive
Growth	Large and mid cap companies	Aggressive
Sector Funds	Industry-specific companies such as biotech or technology	Aggressive
International Funds	International and global companies	Aggressive

Portfolio managers can invest in different size companies to achieve growth. How they define the size is based on what's called "capitalization." Capitalization (caps) is the number of shares that a company has, multiplied by the market price. Mutual funds were created that invest specifically in small caps, medium caps and large caps. Sizes are important to mutual fund investors because they indicate the type of companies and risks associated with them. The rule is: The smaller the capitalization, the greater the risk and the higher the potential for reward. In their infancy, Apple Computer and Microsoft were small caps.

Small cap: a business with $250 million to $1 billion in capitalization. This size might be attractive to investors who want to invest in companies such as Foot Locker Inc. or Longs Drugs.

Medium cap: indicates capitalization of more than $1 billion but less than $5 billion. Includes companies such as Under Armour, American Electric Power, and Urban Outfitters.

Large Cap: indicates capitalization of $5 billion to $250 billion, and includes companies such as Google, Johnson and Johnson, Target, and TJX Companies.

Be advised that there is more risk in investing in funds that specialize in only one of these sizes. Those funds could be affected at the same time by a business or economic cycle. For example, smaller capitalized companies usually have less cash available to weather economic downturns. There is also more risk associated with companies with smaller capitalizations. Remember the market capitalization is calculated by multiplying the number of shares outstanding by the price of the shares. When there are fewer shares outstanding, buyers and sellers can move the price of the shares up or down more easily, which is why these stocks carry more risk. However, small cap stocks have outperformed large cap companies over ten- and twenty-year periods, averaging 12 versus 10 percent. In the short term though, small caps tend to be the most volatile.

You can narrow your focus if you like, and invest in funds that specialize in specific industries. Rather than investing your money in the stock of a technology start-up because you feel it's a good time to invest in technology, you can mitigate some of the risk by investing in a technology sector fund. As you have seen, buying stock in one company could mean losing your entire investment. For example, PSI Net went out of business after the tech boom. Purchasing shares in a mutual fund that invests in a technology sector spreads the risks among several companies. The computer industry has spawned several sector funds under its category, as can be seen in the chart that follows.

TYPES	EXAMPLES
Technology funds	T. Rowe Price Science and Technology
Software funds	Fidelity Select Software and Computer Services
Networking funds	Fidelity Networking and Infrastructure

Step 4. Compile a List of Funds

Look over editors' picks for top-rated mutual funds from publications such as *Kiplinger's Personal Finance* magazine or on the company's website, www.kiplinger.com/investing/kip25. *Money* magazine's seventy top fund selections can be found online at www.cnnmoney.com.

If you are interested in making your own selections, visit www .finance.yahoo.com, which provides screening tailored to your specific criteria. Print out the list and review the recommendations in the *Morningstar Mutual Fund Guide,* available in print or online. Other helpful research tools can be found at Value Line, which provides research and rankings on mutual funds as well as stocks, and at Lipper Analytical, which provides the most extensive of all research and analysis for mutual funds to financial and investment companies. This information is used on sites such as www.cbsmarketwatch.com and www.kiplinger.com, as well as www.thestreet.com.

Step 5. Read the Fine Print on the Prospectus

By law, all mutual funds must state the type of securities the fund manager will invest in. You will find that information in the document called the prospectus. Many investors want to skip this step, but Katherine knew she had to read the fine print because this was the nest egg that would help send her daughters to college eventually. Even though she had narrowed her search, it was still important to make sure the recommendations were a good fit based on the stated objectives.

Take heart, ladies, and know that fund companies are creating more readable prospectuses and the SEC now requires a reader-friendly introductory section. A prospectus may not read like the latest mystery thriller or romance novel, but entertainment is not what we seek by laboring through this exercise. A bright future and a full purse could depend on what is inside those pages. You must know by now that I am an advocate for looking under the hood. Having a Wealthy System requires you to roll up your sleeves so there are no surprises.

The SEC doesn't endorse any investment product, but it works to ensure that the prospectus meets legal requirements. The prospectus not only details the objective of the fund, but also includes information on fees, performance history, the fund manager's resume, and a number of other helpful details that can assist you with making an informed decision.

You will want to get clear on the fund's past performance. When you see a fund's average annual return quoted in the paper or in an advertisement, recognize that the return quoted is based on a certain period of time. Not all investors earned that return because not everyone purchased on December 31 of the prior year, or whatever dates the return represents. And remember that past results are no guarantee of future returns.

Step 6. Determine How Much the Funds Would Cost

Of course you need to know how the price of a mutual fund share is calculated. The price of a mutual fund share is called the "net asset value" or NAV. The NAV is calculated by totaling the value of all the stocks and bonds within the fund at the end of the trading day, and dividing it by the number of shares of the fund that are outstanding. This is simply how the value of your mutual fund shares is determined. You can then multiply the number of shares you own by that price to determine the value of what you own. Mutual fund prices can be found on the investment company's website and are listed in the financial sections of newspapers.

All funds have trading expenses that will vary depending on how much the portfolio is traded or turned over, and advertising costs. Those expenses are all subtracted from the NAV. This is why it is difficult for the average person to understand the overall cost of owning a fund.

Read the prospectus or phone the fund to determine the amount of the management and advertising fees, as trading expenses are reported only after the fact in a fund's annual report. The best number to use for comparison purposes is the expense ratio, which represents the percentage of the fund's assets that go purely toward the expenses of running the fund. The typical expense ratio for a mutual fund is 1.5 percent of the overall assets—this number has been rising. If the fund you are considering is higher than this, you may want to close your purse and look for an alternative.

Purseonality Profile: Sharon deGuzman

A Woman with a Wealthy System

Milwaukee's Sharon deGuzman knows how to set up the most efficient of systems. A fixed-income portfolio manager for Robert W. Baird & Company, she and a team of other investment professionals manage $15 billion in assets for their clients. It's a demanding job, so you can imagine her surprise when she and her husband, Jim, a computer salesman, were trying for a third child and instead learned that they were expecting triplets. According to *The Wall Street Journal,* which chronicled deGuzman's story, mothers generally leave the workforce following multiple births. But deGuzman values her career and giving up her salary was the last thing this couple wanted. They needed a bigger house and car once their family expanded with the premature birth of the triplets in 2005.

What a difference a human capital system can make. More than four dozen of the deGuzmans' relatives, friends, coworkers, church members, and neighbors swung into action, creating a network of support that serves as testimony to the goodwill this couple engendered. A friend coordinated all the volunteers and made assignments according to the times deGuzman indicated that she would need help. One group supplied home-delivered dinners, someone carpooled the youngest daughter to preschool, while others arrived regularly to hold and care for the babies. "People would come over and help put my kids to bed or give one of the babies a bottle," deGuzman told a reporter.

Fourteen weeks after the triplets were born, with the addition of two nannies and help from her father and mother-in-law, deGuzman was able to return to work on a shorter four-day-a-week schedule. The volunteer effort didn't always go like clockwork, but whose does? DeGuzman says she knows that she was blessed. And so are we all, because to some degree, we can create Wealthy Systems of our own.

Purseonality Assessment

DeGuzman's story reminds us to:

Maintain a Social Network. They led busy lives, but the deGuzmans had to have been doing something right for so many people to come to their aid. You, too, will want to keep primary relationships intact, but not because you might need to lean on people. Relationships are hugely important, especially for women. In a 2001 study, researchers at UCLA confirmed what many of us have guessed all along. Rather than the "flight or fight" survivor's mode that men may revert to when agitated, women tend to relieve stress by seeking social contact with other women.

Accept Help When It's Offered. Allowing others to come to her aid was a sign of deGuzman's strength. She not only accepted that she needed help, but seemed to realize that this was a God-given opportunity for community building. Remember that help comes in many forms, including mentors who might guide you to professional success, as well as spouses. If you live with a partner and you don't feel you're getting ample help with child care and housework, find a way to break the impasse, perhaps by seeking professional help. When both individuals work outside the home, their relationship remains more stable when they share child-rearing and household chores.

Make Yourself Irreplaceable at Work. You'll create a network of supportive coworkers if they know they can count on you. When asked about giving deGuzman a more flexible schedule that allowed her to have more time with her expanded family, the president of her firm told a *Wall Street Journal* reporter, "If we can get 50 to 70 percent of an A player's time versus 100 percent of a B player, we will always choose the A player." If you work for someone else, be sure to keep a dialogue going about the goals and priorities your supervisor wants you to focus on.

Step 7. Buy Your Mutual Fund Shares

You've read the fine print and now it's time to purchase the fund. You can place the order by mail, phone, or online in most cases. If this is your first time transacting business with a fund, they will require you to transfer the funds electronically from your bank or savings account or mail a check prior to the purchase. The day you place the order is the *trade date*. You are allowed one day in settlement after the trade date to pay for your trade on the settlement date. The date is when the shares are paid for and ownership is transferred. You will receive a paper (or more than likely an electronic confirmation) the next day, stating the price of your purchased shares and the number of shares purchased. This is vital information that you will need to determine the cost basis at the time you sell. It's important to keep an accurate accounting as you track your future gains and the taxes that will eventually be due. You've completed the process and now it's time to allow your purse to grow and that takes time.

BE SURE TO MONITOR YOUR FUND'S PROGRESS

It's easy to become passive because the investment company and the fund manager make the investing decisions, but stay involved. If you're using an advisor, schedule a telephone checkup every six months. If you're investing on your own, take the time to review the statements you receive quarterly from the investment company.

Compare your fund's performance to the indexes that represent it. For example, if you are invested in an aggressive growth fund with small companies, you would want to know how the Russell 2000 Index has performed over the same time frame.

....

And that's how you, too, can own shares in a mutual fund. Many investors begin with funds and never move on to other kinds of investments. Others view their investments in mutual funds like someone learning to swim. At this point they are only wading in the pool; going into the deep end is akin to investing in individual stocks. You get

I like the Financial Engines site, www.financialengines. com, because it analyzes your portfolio, compares it to your goals, and lets you know if you're on track. The mind behind it is William Sharpe, who was awarded the Nobel Prize in Economics for his modern portfolio theory. There is a small fee attached to the service, but I think it's worth it. Here's how it works:

1. You go to the site and enter the investment products in your portfolio, and your goals. For example, your current portfolio is invested in several mutual funds and you want to retire in twelve years at age fifty-seven.
2. Financial Engines analyzes your portfolio and your goals, and then tells you how close you'll come with your current investment products. It then makes recommendations on specific adjustments you can make to reach your goals, or to at least get you closer to them.

For more details on creating a portfolio, see Pursessentials # 5 on page 238 and # 7 on page 253.

a lot more comfortable in the pool once you learn to swim. As for Dr. Collier, her positive experiences with mutual funds whetted her appetite for diving into the market.

In 1990, she began buying individual stocks. Her biggest pick so far? "I bought Pfizer shares just before the company started selling Viagra." Once stock prices doubled for the pharmaceutical giant, Dr. Collier never looked back. She is now an avid personal investor. I hope your venture into mutual funds will give you the confidence to continue moving ahead, taking one small step for womankind, and a giant leap into the market.

Striking a Balance

In this chapter, Sharon deGuzman demonstrated the female/male strengths of cooperation and taking risks. If the spirit moves you, write about how you envision utilizing these or similar traits to create a wealthy life.

You may want to use some of the following questions as guidelines:

- What risks have I taken lately and how have they paid off?
- What risk have I taken that worked against me but taught me a valuable lesson?
- How have others in my life cooperated for the common good?
- Does being uncooperative ever pay off, and if so, how?

_____

_____

_____

_____

_____

_____

_____

_____

_____

SEVEN | FEATHERING YOUR PURSE FOR RETIREMENT

ALTHOUGH I WILL INTRODUCE MY FINAL WEALTHY Habit in the next chapter, it's important right at this point to explain how you can utilize what you've learned thus far to prepare for retirement. You can draw all those parts together as if you're feathering your nest, which is how Sylvia, a fifty-three-year-old silver-haired public relations executive in Manhattan, explains retirement planning. "I always picture the end result as a robin sitting on a nest, pleased with herself and comfortable. . . . Notice that what I'm leaving out of that picture is the work it takes to get to that point." Sylvia paused to catch her breath. She takes long, vigorous walks during her lunch hour, and today was no exception.

She soon continued, saying, "I tell my friends that no matter how devoted they are to their families, or how busy, or financially stretched to the limit, they owe it to themselves to build that nest while they still have human capital: the energy and drive it takes to earn money so they can save for the future."

I couldn't agree more, which is why this chapter is designed to help you construct a retirement plan, partially by investing. Like Sylvia, I, too, enjoy the enduring image of the nest egg as a symbol for retirement savings, but my vision offers an enhanced edition. I picture a bird nestled in a well-worn, but elegant leather purse that's filled with straw.

Maybe you noticed that I only described one bird in that nest, and not two. Consider it as a reality check. An estimated 51 percent of us currently live without a spouse: this includes those of us who have always been single, lived with partners, or who've been divorced or widowed. There's a likelihood that we'll be on our own.

A neighbor, Janet, a forty-five-year-old executive secretary, has one son about to graduate from college and another who's coming along right behind his brother. Janet confessed that she had saved nothing for retirement. Recently divorced from her husband, she told me, "I had no idea this was coming and he still won't speak to me to tell me what happened." My heart went out to her as we discussed her situation and I was really frank about what lay ahead. When I asked her what I could do to assist her in moving forward financially, she sobbed, but later was grateful when I offered suggestions about what she could do to jump-start her retirement savings.

Far too many women insist on allowing popular culture, which supports the myth that someone else will take care of us, to prevail. Listen up, girlfriends: A man is not a financial plan. What I know to be true is that taking care of ourselves financially is how we reflect our value to others.

One of my close friends, Joyce, has worked for the federal government for twenty years, and she is a shining example of what you can do to keep adding to your purse. At the height of the real estate market in 2006 she sold her townhouse and said, "I am going to rent for a while because I think this housing market is overheated." She took some of the profits and paid off her debt, and then increased the amount she had going into her retirement plans at work.

I suggested that she take advantage of the additional retirement catch-up contributions as well, which she did. Women over the age of fifty can contribute an additional $5,500 to an employer-sponsored plan. She said good naturedly, "I can't afford to take early retirement but I can sure play a mean game of retirement catch up." Joyce is a reminder that it's never too late to fatten your purse.

I have found that many men and women who resist building their nest eggs are so frightened of the idea of growing old that they will not think about that time in their lives. If you ever did think this way, I hope that in boosting your Purseonality Quotient you have developed a whole new attitude about the future. Remember that while it is important for you to be generous to others, you need to save some of your wealth for yourself.

....

As Sylvia continued her noontime walk, she joked that she is so desperate to get other women to listen to her that she's considering standing on a soapbox on a busy corner. "You think women will think I'm crazy if I'm shouting at them, telling them to get ready and that the future is heading straight for them?" In a more serious vein, Sylvia explained that she recently started an investment group for several young women. "No one taught me about the importance of saving for retirement. I had to teach myself, and I didn't want these women to have to look back one day and say the same thing." No soapboxes for me. I'm going to trust in the power of this *Purse* message. If you would like to prepare a nest egg of your own, you'll need to figure out some particulars of what you want and when you'll need it.

VISUALIZING A WEALTHY LIFESTYLE FOR YOUR FUTURE

To consider your life after retirement, avoid generalities such as "I want to live comfortably." This kind of statement is too vague and will not motivate you. Instead, write down specific goals such as:

I want to be in my own home, travel four times a year within the country and abroad annually.

I want to have an ample book-and-garden budget, and be able to afford the food, vitamins, health care, and prescriptions necessary for maintaining excellent health.

I want a car in good shape that can transport me wherever I want to go, and I want to be able to slip small bills to the family when the mood strikes me.

In this manner you'll be creating your wealthy lifestyle plan, even if only in rough draft. What is your plan for becoming a wealthy woman? Rewrite that list and continue to get clearer on what you want. Putting your dreams into your purse will make you more confident that you know where you're going.

ESTIMATE HOW MUCH YOU NEED
TO PUT IN YOUR PURSE

If you cleaned out your purse in the first chapter, you may have most of the information needed to answer these questions. Now you will want to come up with a price tag for retirement.

- How much time do you estimate that it will take you to become financially independent?
- How much do you currently earn each year?
- How much of your current annual earnings are you willing to commit?
- How much have you already accumulated in savings, investments, and retirement plans?
- How much do you regularly add to those investments?
- Do your investments match the return you need or are you invested too conservatively?

Let's say that you're thirty-five now and want to be leading a wealthy lifestyle by age fifty-five. That gives you twenty years. According to statistics, on average women live to about age eighty-five. But let's say that people in your family tend to live longer. If you don't smoke, don't drink heavily, eat a healthy diet, and exercise regularly, your life expectancy might be about ninety. That would mean building a purse that lasts, so figure out your own unique time line.

Prioritize your lifestyle and estimate how much you'll need. When you stop working, you will no longer be saving for retirement, paying payroll tax, commuter costs, and buying work clothes. But unless you have excellent health care benefits that will follow you into retirement, you will probably have to pay increased health insurance costs. Let's say that you currently make $50,000 a year. The general estimate is that you'll need around 80 percent of your prior income to maintain your standard of living after you stop working. Let's make a more conservative assumption and say that you'll need 90 percent. That works out to $40,000.

You can work out a budget for yourself. The task will be easier if you already know how much you spend now. If you've cleaned out your purse, you know your net worth, you've created a budget, and should have a ballpark estimate of your needs. If you have some expensive goals, such as travel, be sure to include them in your budget. If you have already itemized your expenses, look over them and determine what you will likely be continuing after you stop working.

INFLATION FACTOR

After estimating how much you need annually, project your estimated income at an inflation-adjusted rate of 4 percent. You may be aiming for the equivalent of $50,000 a year when you retire in twenty-five years. At 4 percent inflation, that $50,000 today is the same as $133,000 when you retire. Before you get caught up in that number, think of how crazy it would have sounded in 1972, when we paid eight cents for a first-class stamp, to say we'd be paying forty-four cents today. The concept of continually rising prices can help you understand why 4 percent annual inflation during a twenty-five-year retirement can reduce the value of a $1,000 pension check to just $375. You can calculate your retirement needs as adjusted for inflation at www .kiplinger.com/businessresource/tools/inflation.html.

When you have finished calculating how much you need to fund your vision, write that figure here. In the financial world, it is referred to as "your number."

Please write your number here $ _____

If that figure leaves you gasping, take a deep breath. One of the confusing aspects of retirement planning in the United States is that there is no unified plan. You have to put together one piece from here, another piece from there. Come to think of it, this process sounds like you're building a nest that can withstand unexpected storms. Here are the three most important components that you will need:

- Tax-deferred retirement savings plans
- Employee-funded individual retirement accounts
- Social Security.

TAX-DEFERRED RETIREMENT SAVINGS PLANS

If you work for a company or organization that offers a tax-deferred retirement plan and haven't signed up, pull off those spike heels and run as fast as you can to join. With some employer-sponsored plans, money is deducted from your salary referred to as your "contribution." Depending on your job, you may have access to one of the following:

401(k): available to employees of corporations

403(b): available to employees of nonprofit organizations, such as universities and charitable organizations

457(b): available to some employees of state and local governments

TSP: available to civilian employees of the federal government and the armed services

By the way, if you own a small business, you can set up a Keogh (pronounced KEY-oh) or if you are your sole employee, Solo-401(k)s are available. Despite the weird letters and numbers, these are some of the sexiest deals going, generating growth through investments of your choosing.

When I left Fidelity Investments, I was ecstatic at the amount of money in my 401(k). My contributions of the maximum amount allowed of 12 percent of my salary, along with my employer's 50 percent match up to 6 percent of my salary, spurred a phenomenal impact on my overall return. Those retirement savings later provided the safety net that gave me the confidence and sense of security I needed to step out and start my own business.

With your 401(k)-type plan, you get investment gains without paying any tax on them at the time, because the taxes are deferred until you withdraw from these accounts. If your company matches your contribution dollar-for-dollar (usually up to about 6 percent), that works out to receiving the equivalent of a 100-percent return on your investment.

Here's how the matches work. Some employers offer a fifty-cent match on each contributed dollar up to the first 6 percent. So if you earn $50,000 annually and contribute $3,000 (6 percent) you will receive a 50 percent return, an extra $1,500. I don't know about you, but if I'm offered free money, I take it. This is how my retirement account grew so quickly.

You should contribute at least the maximum your employer is willing to match. Anything less is like throwing away money, which is a criminal offense in my book. It's disheartening to hear that an esti-mated one third of workers with 401(k)-type plans don't invest enough to qualify for the full company match. That figure rises to two thirds of workers when it comes to those earning less than $25,000 a year. Twenty-eight percent of eligible employees don't even sign up for their company plans.

If you decide to leave your job, you get to keep your own con-tributions and those gains. To keep the money your employer gives you, you have to become vested, a term that describes gaining lifetime membership to an employer's retirement program. After a company has employed you for a certain number of years, you become vested and get to keep the company's contributions, too. Each 401(k) plan has different rules about when an employee becomes vested.

....

The vesting schedule you're offered will be "cliff" or "graded." A cliff-vesting schedule involves one length of time. Once you've been with the company for that stated period you're vested. For instance, with a three-year cliff-vesting schedule, after three years of service you're vested. If you quit with two years and 364 days—one day short of that year—you're not vested. With graded vesting, you become progressively more vested each year. For example, with a four-year graded vesting schedule, you become 25 percent vested each year. After four years, you are fully vested.

Sylvia viewed her retirement plan as such a good deal that although she was reeling after her husband died from a stroke in 1996, she opted to sock away more tax-deferred money than her employer matched. "I had to make a lot of tough decisions to justify it, but I don't regret it. The nice thing about having the money deducted automatically is that you don't think about it, and the money grows quietly, while you're looking the other way." Although this was an unmatched contribution, she still qualified for a tax deduction and tax-deferred growth.

Sylvia earns $100,000. Her employer match of 6 percent gave her $6,000 in addition to the $6,000 she contributed, which added $12,000 a year in tax-deferred savings. But Sylvia contributed another 6 percent, $6,000, which brought her total annual contribution up to $18,000. Her fund grew through compounding and reinvestment.

After Sylvia taught herself about investment basics, she began making decisions about how and where her money would be invested. "I'm a pretty conservative investor," she says. "I'm definitely not into high risk. That meant that my retirement fund didn't grow as fast as I might have liked, but those conservative investments did buffer me when many of my colleagues lost about half of what they'd had. I didn't come up with a sound portfolio on my own. I conferred with a financial advisor that my company hired for us."

She's not alone in benefiting from these employer-sponsored advisors. One study found that when employees have this kind of professional advice, they earn an extra 3 percent on their accounts each year. That may sound minimal initially, but as it compounds over the years, we're talking tens of thousands of dollars difference. Over the course of your career, losing one percentage point of annual return on your 401(k)-type portfolio can reduce the size of your fund by 20 percent. If you're too busy to handle your account, and consider hiring a manager from an outside firm, be prepared to pay fees that can run as high a full percentage point a year, in addition to what mutual fund managers are already charging you.

By managing your own 401(k)-type account and checking periodically to ensure that your investments are efficient and age appropriate—and balanced—you can check to see whether you have invested too conservatively for your time horizon and only earning minimal returns. Conversely, if you're nearing retirement, whether you've invested too aggressively.

You will need a mix of stock and bond mutual funds, based on your retirement date. Many employers are increasingly assigning participating employees to target-date funds, which shuffles a mix of stocks, bonds, and cash based on an employee's planned retirement date.

Regular 401(k) contributions also allow you the benefits of dollar-cost-averaging, which allows you to buy more shares during a bear market, and fewer when it is up. Once the bull returns, those additional shares will yield bigger gains.

BUYER BEWARE: KNOW THE RULES FOR YOUR 401(K)-TYPE PLAN

TRY NOT TO DISTURB THAT MONEY

The government tries to discourage workers under the age of 59½ from withdrawing money from tax-advantaged funds by charging you big-time if you try to cash out. And you may pay that high price even if you mistakenly move these funds from one retirement account to another.

Here's what I mean: You leave a job, and after starting a new one, want to transfer your 401(k) funds to the new account. The safest way to handle this transaction is to have the money moved from one qualified retirement account to another through a "direct rollover." This is exactly what I instructed Fidelity to do when I left the company. With a rollover, the money is sent from one tax-advantaged account to the next, or you deliver the money personally in a check that has been made payable by your old retirement account custodian to the next one. If you don't explain it's a direct rollover and the check is made out to you and deposited into your personal account first, you could pay steep fees. If you actually receive the funds, you have sixty days from the distribution date to roll over the funds into an IRA rollover account to avoid any taxes or penalties.

Even before you receive a check, the plan sponsor can withhold as much as 24 percent off the top. That amount includes a 10 percent penalty for early distribution, 10 percent in an advance federal tax payment, and the rest for state taxes, which vary. If someone in the 25 percent tax bracket withdraws $10,000 from a 401(k)-type fund, she will wind up with about $6,500, and maybe less, depending on state taxes.

WATCH THOSE LOANS

You are allowed by law to borrow from your 401(k) plan—typically $50,000 or half of your vested balance, with highly favorable interest rates—but failure to repay on time can result in a 10 percent excise tax, *and* you will have to pay state and federal income tax. A severe hit to your savings in the long run. A study released by the Center for American Progress found that a $5,000 loan could cut your retirement savings by as much as 22 percent, even if you repay the loan without penalty. If you want to find out how much a 401(k)-type loan will cost you over time? Do the math on the Standard & Poors calculator at www.fc.standardandpoors.com/srl/srl_v35/calculators .jsp?catid=000007.

EMPLOYEE-FUNDED INDIVIDUAL RETIREMENT ACCOUNTS

If you have earned income and don't have access to a 401(k)-type plan, *or* you can afford to set aside additional retirement funds, consider opening a Roth or a traditional IRA at a financial institution such as a bank, credit union, or brokerage house. With both these accounts your contributions are invested, but there are significant differences between the traditional and Roth IRA. With the traditional you can make tax-deductible contributions. With the Roth, you don't get tax-free benefits until you're 59½ or have owned it for at least five years. Both are subject to income limits in order to qualify to make a contribution.

When I left Fidelity, I didn't stop investing in my future. I knew all too well what happens when you lose the one thing money can't buy: time. I opened a TIAA-CREF Growth and Income Individual Retirement Account (IRA) and funded it with the money I earned from speaking and consulting. I didn't want to keep all my nest egg at Fidelity and ventured out into other investment companies. Of course, my income had dropped considerably and there wasn't a lot of extra income, but I had reduced my expenses considerably. No more live-in nanny, commuting expenses like parking, gas and the cost of lunches, expensive suits and dry cleaning. My office was set up in the spare bedroom in the basement. I had a telephone line installed and shared it with the fax—and Owens Media Group LLC was up and running. The first year I was able to contribute $1,000 to my IRA, and the following year I contributed the maximum, $2,000.

What a difference a few years make. The limits of what you can contribute to both the traditional and Roth IRAs have more than doubled, and the amounts increase every year. By 2008 you could contribute as much as $5,000 to a traditional IRA and deduct that amount from your taxes when you file the following year. You don't have to pay taxes on that money until it is withdrawn.

If you withdraw money from the traditional IRA before the age of 59½ you will have to pay state and federal taxes and a 10 percent penalty. Most important, at age 70½ you will have to adhere to a "required minimum distribution" rule that requires you to withdraw minimal amounts from the account, or you will have to pay an excess accumulation tax. A lot of people get tripped up on this rule and lose money with traditional IRAs. Most workers who opt for the traditional IRA don't have an employer-sponsored plan or are looking for an up-front tax break.

I admit it; even though there are no upfront tax savings, the Roth IRA is my favorite of the two for a number of reasons:

- There are no annual withdrawal requirements with a Roth. When you do make withdrawals, any time after you are 59½, those withdrawals are tax-free.

- If you've had a Roth account open for five years or more and want to buy a new home, you can withdraw as much as $10,000 without having to pay penalties or taxes, on your earnings.

- You can withdraw earnings from a Roth to pay for your own or a dependent child's college expenses.

- A Roth allows you to save for college and retirement simultaneously. If you can afford to leave the money in place after retirement, it can continue to grow tax-free.

INCOME RESTRICTIONS FOR IRAS

To be eligible for a Roth, your taxable income had to be under $116,000 (as a single taxpayer) or $169,000 (as a married taxpayer filing jointly) in 2008. For the traditional IRA, income limits were $85,000 to 105,000 for married couples, widows, or widowers in 2008. If you were a single taxpayer or head of household your income had to be more than $53,000 but less than $63,000. If you're a spouse filing separately, your income had to be less than $10,000; a nonworking spouse can make a deductible contribution of $5,000 if the adjusted gross income doesn't exceed $156,000. Since these figures are subject to change, check with your tax accountant or with a financial advisor for current IRA income restrictions.

As my income from the business increased, I also established a SEP-IRA (simplified employee pension) plan and a personal 401(k) that allowed me to increase the percentage I could contribute, and gave me access to the same type of benefits as if I had remained with Fidelity.

SOCIAL SECURITY

I intentionally left Social Security for last because it should be considered as a complement to your nest egg as opposed to its foundation. While you may have seen attention-grabbing headlines that warned of the end of this program, rest easy. These benefits, financed from payroll taxes of current workers, does require some government retooling to meet the strain of more than 77 million baby boomers who will be retiring in coming decades, but the system is not broken.

If you are twenty-five or older and receiving annual Social Security statements (see the end of this paragraph for information on how to request your statement), look at the amount you are scheduled to receive, based on your earnings record, when you retire. These figures will be adjusted with cost-of-living increases. Multiply that annual amount by the number of years you expect to live in retirement. For instance, someone receiving $1,600 a month or $19,200 a year is scheduled to receive $480,000 over twenty-five years. If you're not receiving this statement, you can request a copy online at www.socialsecurity. gov or by phoning the Social Security Administration at (800) 772-1213.

You can subtract this amount from the number you estimated that you would need overall to fund a comfortable retirement. If you need $1 million, and you'll be getting $480,000 over your lifetime, that covers a little less than half of what you need.

Unless you have compromised health, you may well be advised by a financial advisor to delay applying for early Social Security benefits, because you will receive a lower benefit, which means less money over your lifetime. Your Social Security statement will offer a determination, according to your birth date, of when you qualify for early or normal retirement.

A University of Pennsylvania study found that a baby boomer earning a final salary of $75,000 might receive about $1,320 a month by taking an early retirement at age sixty-two. But by waiting until age seventy, that same boomer would get $2,884 monthly, more than twice as much.

....

There are of course other components that you can add to your nest egg.

Traditional pensions: The amount received is based on the number of years you've worked for an employer. If you qualify for this benefit, and do not already have an updated statement, ask your human resources department for help in determining the amount of your payout.

Individual annuities: These self-funded pensions work like life insurance policies in reverse. You hand over a certain amount of money to an insurance company, which invests the money and then at retirement pays you a monthly allowance as long as you live. As with all major financial contracts, you will want to check with an independent financial advisor before signing. You will find plenty of helpful information on these policies by reading *Kiplinger's Personal Finance* or *Money* magazines.

Liquid assets and your investment portfolio: Keeping cash on hand is always extremely important, and hopefully by the time you retire you will have built up a substantial savings and holdings in mutual funds and personal investments.

By the time you've established an investment portfolio with employment-sponsored and individual retirement accounts and figured out how much you'll have coming in through Social Security and/or pension benefits, you will be well on your way to having put together a nest egg that can keep money flowing in for the rest of your life, no matter how long that may be.

KEEP YOUR NEST EGG INTACT WITH INSURANCE

Your nest egg can be secured if you purchase insurance. Sylvia's husband died without insurance, and as a result, she figures that she will have to work until she is well into her seventies to afford a comfortable retirement. She says, "We had a lot of plans. I never realized until Ted was gone that life insurance is not a luxury but a necessity."

While there are many types of life insurance contracts, they basically boil down to two: permanent and term. Permanent life insurance remains in effect for the life of the policyholder, as long as agreed-upon payments are made. It tends to be the most expensive type of life insurance. Term insurance covers a policyholder for a period of one to thirty years, and is far more affordable than permanent.

The most common reason for purchasing life insurance is to replace the income of a family member whom others depend on. Financial advisors suggest that you multiply your annual salary by a factor of ten or twenty and then buy that amount of term life insurance for a period that will cover you until you retire. But as we women know, one-size-fits-all rarely compares to having something tailored to our needs. You can accomplish this by conducting an insurance needs analysis to customize what amount of death benefits your family requires. Visit my website at www.deborahowens.com to link to a life insurance estimator.

Striking a Balance

In this chapter, Sylvia demonstrated the female/male strengths of empathy and independence. If the spirit moves you, write about how you envision utilizing these or similar traits to create a wealthy life.

You may want to use some of the following questions as guidelines:

- Why does caring for other people matter when it comes to investing?
- What does it mean to have empathy for myself?
- If I want to become/remain financially independent, what do I need to do?
- Why is independence one of the most valued traits in wealthy thinking?

_____

_____

_____

_____

_____

_____

_____

_____

_____

EIGHT | PASSING ON WHAT YOU'VE LEARNED

WEALTHY HABIT #7: LEGACY

OVER THE YEARS I'VE GROWN ACCUSTOMED TO SEE-ing mothers showing up with their daughters at my "Purse of Your Own" workshops. Many of the women have told me that they were determined that their daughters would enter the adult world thinking like wealthy women, and, hopefully, avoid some of the financial mistakes they had made. I understand where they're coming from. There are things that I wish my mother had been able to share with me about relationships and money. Terry and I have worked hard to teach Brandon and Olivia to aim high financially, but, of course, children are influenced not only by their parents, but also by messages promulgated in the media about how everyone is expected to live.

So even though I come from the school of looking good for less, by the time Olivia was thirteen, she refused to walk inside my favorite discount store. I didn't force the issue—I knew better. The one time that I had insisted that she just look through the racks at a local bargain store, she was not subtle and was quick to make her opinions known: "I don't want to shop here. This is where they send the clothes nobody else wants."

While she might not like the discount stuff, she is into the "casual luxury" clothing that was much on display when we traveled to New York a while back along with other teenagers who were studying modern dance. After watching a performance, the children railroaded us parents into visiting a brand-new store crammed with what looked like six floors of ripped jeans and faded see-through T-shirts. Terry picked up one that featured letters hanging by threads, and was speechless when he looked at the price tag: one hundred and fifty smackeroos.

Some of the other parents were frowning, too, but they pulled out their credit cards and joined the line of shoppers waiting to pay. Terry looked at me with an expression that said, "I *know* you are not buying this child any clothes in here." He seemed to have forgotten that since Olivia works for her money, she can spend it on anything within reason that she desires, provided that she tithe, save, or invest half of it. And just minutes later, she reminded me that children do watch and learn from the behaviors we model.

I tried not to look smug as Olivia and I left the store without spending a dime. She was developing a Wealthy Vision. She saw what she wanted during that trip all right, but it wasn't hanging on a clothes rack. Weeks later, after receiving another paycheck, Olivia researched information on clothing companies in the youth market, found two that looked financially sound and were selling at affordable prices, and put her love for casual luxury clothing to work by purchasing shares from the retailers Abercrombie & Fitch and Aeropostale.

It wouldn't be fair to set her up as a paragon. In months and years to come, Olivia will surely succumb to the lure of the marketplace and pay too much for items that the media and society are branding as the next "must haves." Few of us, especially the young, have the steely discipline that allows us to always march past a store because (a) we can't afford it, or (b) it's not worth the asking price. I trust, though, that their vision will take them far beyond moments of immediate gratification. I would hope that during their lives, they realize that with wealth comes the responsibility of teaching others how to create wealth. If I leave them nothing else this would be my most important legacy.

WEALTHY HABIT # 7: A WEALTHY LEGACY

A Wealthy Legacy is about investing in others. This habit promotes the importance of paying your way forward. To receive, you must first give something of value. People who develop this habit recognize that it is in giving that they receive, and they relish the opportunity to leave a path for others to follow.

Women teaching girls about money is an especially vital mission in a world in which so many are still raised with the unconscious notion that having a man and having financial security is one and the same. Growing up, they might have been told that they can be anything, and yet they are barraged with images of animated princesses awakened by knights in shining armor. There is nothing wrong with being a princess if you are next in line to rule the empire. This is the legacy that *Purse* bestows on women and their daughters. I suggest that you create your own fairy tales and insert the stories of women that you've read about in *Purse* to provide your daughters with insight on romance and finance. Let's share the stories of powerful women who know how to grow a mean purse.

If you have a daughter, I hope you will tell them of Grammy Hall of Fame singer Judy Collins, who for twenty years let her male business manager handle all of her finances, until she discovered that he hadn't even left her enough to pay her taxes. Collins has since said that like many women, she was raised to believe in rescue fantasies and lulled into inaction with the promise that a prince would come. Collins tells other women, "I'm here to tell you . . . no one is coming."

The lives of your daughters, little sisters, granddaughters, and nieces will be so much better if they can be convinced that no one is coming to rescue them. The good news is that they can create wealth on their own.

Across the nation, a number of wealthy women have devoted much of their time to teaching children about the importance of investing. Let me tell you about just three women who are paying it forward for girls and boys.

Muriel Siebert, a college dropout who in 1967 became one of the first women to join 1,365 male brokers (at a cost of $445,000) with a seat on the New York Stock Exchange, helps pay the bill for New York City students to learn financial literacy.

In Detroit, Gail Perry-Mason, a vice president for Oppenheimer Investments, donates $10,000 each summer, and manages and teaches at Money Matters for Youth, a summer camp for inner city students. She says, "I think this is the best investment I'll ever make."

And in Chicago, Mellody Hobson, a Princeton University graduate and *Good Morning America* contributor who worked her way up from intern to president at Ariel Capital Management, a money management firm, put her full support behind the Ariel Elementary

If you're interested in starting a financial literacy/investment class at your child's school, try working through the PTA. And if you're interested in enrolling your child in a financial literacy/investing summer camp, here are a few names and Web addresses of camps that were featured in *The Wall Street Journal*.

Camp Millionaire: www.creativewealthintl.org/campmillionaire.php

YoungBiz: www.youngbiz.com/Florida/index.html

Camp Challenge: www.campsertoma.org/camp/challengee.html

Young Americans Center for Financial Education: www.yacenter.org

Community Academy. Incoming first-grade classes are given $20,000 that the children ultimately invest in stocks.

Of course, you don't have to fund a school to teach girls about the importance of investing; start at home. I met one woman from Boston, Lorraine, a restaurant manager, who said she helped her fourteen-year-old line up weekend babysitting jobs on the condition that she would contribute some of her earnings to a Roth IRA. "She is only contributing about $500 a year, but as I told her, it's not the amount she's saving, but the value of what she's learning about investing for the future. Now one of her friends is opening an account." And Ernestine, a grandmother in Richmond, Virgina, said that she hosts "finance weekends" for her five grandchildren who range in age from twelve to seventeen. "It's like a sleepover at grandma's. And before we start the all-night videos and pass around popcorn and Twizzlers, they help me decide how they want me to invest the money I'm putting into their custodial investment accounts."

Purseonality Profile: Liz Ann Sonders

A Woman with a Wealthy Legacy

Like so many folks, Liz Ann Sonders started college without really knowing what she wanted to do, and then her father intervened. In the 1980s, Sonders was an economics major at the University of Delaware with an interest in political science. One evening Sonders's father convinced her to watch a TV investment show with him, and she fell for the stock market. "I love talking about investing," she said. "I love the subject matter. On a vacation I'd choose to sit in a beach chair and read *The Economist*."

From that point, she focused on building a career in investing, earning a master's in business administration from Fordham University, working up to portfolio manager at an institutional fund, and then serving high net–worth investors. In 2002, she was named chief investment strategist, a newly created position, for Charles Schwab, a financial services firm that manages $1.4 trillion in assets.

Her job requires her to pass on what she knows.

Sonders keeps apprised of what's occurring in the United States and overseas markets so she can offer long-term investment advice to her company's 7.2 million brokerage account clients and 13,400 employees through company communications. If that were Sonders's only job, she'd be more than busy enough.

But since this skillful communicator is comfortable stating her opinions, she is much in demand. Making her busier still, Sonders takes day trips around the United States and travels overseas twice a year, often for speaking engagements. Ever poised, speaking with clarity and confidence, she is quoted frequently in the major media and appears on financial programs such as CNBC's *Street Signs* and Fox News' *Your World with Neil Cavuto*.

Such a demanding career might easily distract her from other aspects of her life, but this wife and the mother of two, ages eight and eleven, somehow stays on track. She and her husband own two homes. The one in Darien, Connecticut, was built as a mid-nineteenth-century hunting lodge. During the week her parents look after the children, but on Fridays Sonders works at home so she can be there when they return from school, and so she can drive them to their activities or out for an afternoon treat. She did take up golf again, but only after her children grew big enough to ride in the carts.

Given her schedule, you would think she'd sound frantic, but on a busy Friday morning, after getting her children off to school, she couldn't have sounded more relaxed. Her advice to investors is to focus on the long-term and to not get distracted by market fluctuations. "In 1960, the average investor held stock for eight years; now it's ten months. So we are way too short-term oriented as investors, and this is driven by a constant flow of Internet information. At the click of a button we are barraged with information about temporary stock fluctuations about changes in ownership, and it's killing us as investors."

Sonders is grateful when she hears about people who are taking her advice, and adds that one of her most meaningful encounters with an investor occurred in Naples, Florida, after she'd given a speech. "A woman who appeared to be in her fifties introduced herself. She said that she'd started watching me on television years before and that she still tries to catch me when I'm on. She's a Schwab customer and reads the reports I write for the company." This woman told Sonders that she had never lost sight of her message, that when she was frightened about her investments, to take a deep breath and stay focused on the long term. Sonders said the woman added, "I want you to know that I did. I used to work as a police officer, but I was able to retire at forty-eight. Thank you."

Focusing on the long-term has worked for Sonders. The girl who once had no idea where she was going is now a woman who's right where she wants to be.

Purseonality Assessment

Sonders's story can remind you to:

Show Your Daughter What It's Like to Have a Passion for Work. If you aren't doing something you love, point to other women who are. And show by example that it's worth making sacrifices—going to night school for retraining, if necessary—so you can get that job you love.

Help Her Start an Investment Club. She and her friends will learn to turn their knowledge concerning name brands into profits.

Listen to Her. Pay attention when she speaks. Of course you're often too busy to stop and make sure you're getting her point, but maybe if you slow down, you will convince her that what she has to say is important.

Children seldom listen to lectures, of course, and I'm sure you know that modeling Wealthy Habits is one of the surest routes for sending girls in the right direction. To that end, help her get her little purse together by utilizing a few of the suggestions that follow.

FROM HER EARLIEST DAYS

PREPARE HER WAY

If someone offers to host a baby shower, suggest that guests contribute to a mutual fund in your daughter's name with you as the trustee. Have the checks written to you if your newborn has not yet arrived. To establish the mutual fund you will need a Social Security number for a minor. Visit www.ssa.gov to obtain a Social Security number application and to find their nearest office locations.

GIVE THE GIFT THAT KEEPS ON GIVING

For birthdays or Christmas, gift a share of stock at www.oneshare .com. My First Stock kids own shares in companies they can relate to, such as Disney, McDonald's, and Mattel. The site allows you to select companies that are appropriate for their age group. Purchase a stock of your choice, then personalize it by adding an engraved message, a custom matte, and one of many gorgeous frames. Adorn their room with stock certificates and be assured that dividends will be paid forward into their future.

TEACH HER TO USE MONEY WISELY

Instead of a piggy bank, pick up four purses from a 99-cent store and mark one for "spending," another for "saving," and the others for "sharing" and "investing." When coins fill the savings purse, help her open a savings account. She can use her "investing" money to contribute to a mutual fund that may already be opened in her name. Her sharing money might be spent on helping those less fortunate. As for the "spending" purse, she may not require any help in figuring that one out.

SHOP LIKE AN INVESTOR

While she's still young enough to enjoy shopping with you, comment in ways that she can understand about companies that you would consider for investments. For instance, "I like cereals by Kellogg's, and that company has been in business for a long time. I want to take a look at their stock prices."

INVEST IN HIGHER EDUCATION

Open and discuss a 529 plan with her. These savings plans offer tax advantages and encourage saving for future college costs. They can include stocks and shifted down to less risky investments as college nears. For more information on these plans, refer to Pursessential # 9 on page 267.

AGE SEVEN AND UP

RAISE HER FINANCIAL LITERACY

Make bread or rolls with yeast and as the dough rises, explain that compound interest expands in a similar manner. You invest something and then you earn something on your initial investment, and as you continue to earn money on top of your money, it may be hard to see the difference at first, but then it continues to expand as if a miracle is occurring.

CHANGE HER STORY

Rewrite fairy tales as you read aloud to her. Have some fun with these. Cinderella, for instance, could marry her handsome prince but then open her own shoe business. Gretel (in *Hansel and Gretel*) could convince the evil witch to open a bakery. If you don't feel up to this challenge, read the story as it is and engage your daughter afterward with a gentle discussion about what the heroine might have done if she was going to become an independent woman.

HOST A "TAKE YOUR DAUGHTER TO THE STREET" DAY

On Take Our Daughters to Work Day, invite her and some friends on an outing to a regional stock market. Explain that with investments, your money works for you.

AGE TWELVE AND UP

OPEN AN INVESTMENT ACCOUNT

For a birthday, give your daughter the gift of choice. Tell her she's old enough to find and research a company that reflects her interests, with companies such as Walt Disney, for instance. You can support her in her choices and introduce her to www.sharebuilder.com, since it has no minimum investment, no account minimum, and no inactivity fee. The company will even allow her to buy fractional shares, in case she's interested in investing a fixed amount monthly.

TEACH HER TO INVEST WITH OTHER KIDS

Volunteer with a teacher at her school to establish a Stock Market Game* competition. Starting with a virtual cash account of $100,000, students strive to create the best-performing portfolio using a live trading simulation. They work together in teams practicing leadership, organization, negotiation, and cooperation as they compete to win the top spot. It is an engaging exercise that merges young people's love of computers and games to garner their attention and interest. The end result is a rich learning experience with real-life applications.

TEACH HER TO INVEST IN HER VALUES

Discuss with her the importance of finding investments that are in keeping with what she cares about. To that end, she might want to contact USAA First Start Growth at (800) 531-8448, a fund that accepts low monthly automatic payments and attracts young investors by offering a mix of stocks that exclude tobacco, alcohol, and gambling interests.

REWARD HER FOR DELAYING GRATIFICATION

As a holiday gift, give her a $50 bill and tell her that if she can hold on to that for a year, you will give her a $100 bill in its place. Or take it one step further by matching dollar amounts that she puts away toward longer term goals like her first car. Establish a mutual fund ac-

---

* The Stock Market Game is a trademark of the Foundation for Investor Education, a nonprofit organization dedicated to developing and providing learning resources for investors of all ages. Visit www.stockmarketgame.org.

count in her name and transfer a set monthly amount between $20 and $50 from her savings account. This type of commitment can assist her in pursuing part-time jobs such as babysitting or waiting tables to insure that she has the funds available for her monthly commitment. See Pursessential # 9 on page 267 for information on establishing an automatic account builder for a minor.

BOOST HER READING SKILLS

Show her stock listings in the newspaper and discuss companies that may be familiar to her. Ask her to visit the company's website and obtain a copy of their annual report. After she reads the report, ask her questions about the state of the company. Are they earning money and are they profitable? Do you think this company would make a good investment? Show her how to read the company's financial statements and relate it to the family's finances. The statement of cash flow can be related to your check register, and you can share the net worth exercise in Chapter One to explain balance sheets in the annual report.

CUT AND PASTE HER WAY TO WEALTH

Help her put together a scrapbook of the companies she would like to buy with current stock prices listed beside them. The more creative you make this exercise, the more interest she will show. Help her search in magazines for pictures and advertisements of the company's products. She can paste used gift cards from her favorite store or other items to add dimension to the presentation. Have her write a short narrative on the company and why she believes the company would be a good investment on the scrapbook page. This is also a great exercise for Purse Groups.

TEACH HER THE DOWNSIDE OF COMPOUNDING

When you pay your bills, invite your daughter to sit beside you. Explain how compound interest can work against those who don't pay bills in a timely fashion, and also how debt can weigh people down.

YOUNG ADULTS

INTRODUCE HER TO A ROTH

As she earns money from summer jobs, encourage her to open a Roth IRA. This is an excellent way for young people to start saving because they can have access to the money from their original investment without penalties after five years to purchase a home or for higher education expenses.

SHOP FOR COLLEGES

When she begins looking at colleges, help her to look for those that offer the best value, institutions that offers high-quality education at an affordable price. If she has her eye on a private or Ivy League institution, encourage her to look for scholarships. Many of the corporations that she may have researched as stock investments have foundations that offer scholarships to high-achieving students. Her honed research skills will come in handy as she pursues higher education.

....

As your daughter grows into a young woman with an investing eye, you will be so grateful that you raised someone with street smarts—Wall Street smarts, that is.

Striking a Balance

Liz Ann Sonders's story exemplifies the female/male strengths of curiosity and confidence. If the spirit moves you, write about how you envision utilizing these or similar traits to create a wealthy life.

You may want to consider some of the following questions as guidelines:

- What are the subjects that I can never seem to learn enough about?
- How might I use my curiosity to improve my life?
- How does the saying "Curiosity killed the cat and satisfaction brought him back" apply to a situation in my life?
- How do I go about getting what I need to be confident?
- What subject am I able to weigh in on with total confidence?
- Why is confidence necessary in my pursuit of wealth?

_____

_____

_____

_____

_____

_____

_____

_____

_____

NINE | UTILIZING THE
7 WEALTHY HABITS IN CONCERT

Up to now I've presented the 7 Wealthy Habits separately. My aim was to help you become more like a musician, learning to play one new movement at a time and then all of them together. You can do the same with the Wealthy Habits. Like real estate broker Claudia Coonrad Barnette of McClean, Virginia, you can learn to utilize all seven Wealthy Habits in concert.

Barnette wasn't born into wealth, but she had great role models who helped her to acquire the habits and attitudes described throughout this book. She told me, "When I was a girl, my grandfather used to have me read the stock pages and that is my first memory of the stock market and investing." I met Barnette when she and her husband answered a casting call for *My Generation*, a TV show produced by AARP and broadcast through ComCast Cable, where I played a "wealth coach." After the segment was produced I convinced her to share her story with you.

As a child she spent summers in upstate New York with her grandparents. Afternoons her granddad taught her that she could find the world of businesses represented in the daily financial section of the newspaper in the stock section. He instilled her with confidence, never suggesting that she was too young to master a subject that some adults considered complicated. She says, "He taught me what it meant when stock prices rose and fell." In this manner she developed a Wealthy Outlook.

A WEALTHY OUTLOOK: This foundational habit offers a macro or "big picture" view of the world. It is a habit that encourages adding value. It is characteristic of successful people and a core value of great companies, allowing them to move beyond boundaries.

Her grandfather had already infused Barnette's mother with a passion for investing, so when her grandparents passed away, her mother parlayed the $25,000 in proceeds from their estate into a significant portfolio. Barnette says of her homemaker-investor mother, "Every stock she purchased was dividend paying, and she reinvested those dividends." Barnette's mother stayed in the market for decades, refusing to be intimidated by economic downturns. How powerful is that purse, sisters? She served as living proof that when it comes to investing, the playing field is level. By the time of her death, Barnette's mother turned her $25,000 inheritance into a $2.5 million portfolio. She says of her mom, "Twelve hours before she passed away, she was watching CNBC—and she was bedridden in an oxygen tent. At her funeral, a broker told me that my mother was the wisest investor he had ever known." Barnette's mother had surely developed a Wealthy Focus.

A **WEALTHY FOCUS** helps you to remain determined, set priorities, and eliminate distractions as you pursue goals. Wealthy people recognize that stating specific desired outcomes allows them to stay on course.

With these kinds of role models, it only made sense for Barnette to be attracted to someone with her grandfather's characteristics, right? Wrong! Not only was her first husband not interested in investing, or saving, for that matter: "He didn't pay bills and as long as he had money coming in he didn't worry." The couple divorced eventually, but not before Barnette's confidence had been shaken. "I thought I would become a homeless person or a bag lady."

Barnette looked to herself for answers. Why wouldn't she? This was the daughter of a homemaker who placed stock orders over the phone during the 1960s, when there was no access to easy research and investment purchases via the Internet. You won't be surprised to learn that rather than becoming a bag lady, Barnette prospered. A Wealthy Vision helped her identify her own unique talents.

She became a real estate developer and broker and sold high-end condos and homes to the wealthy. And then, talk about paying it forward! Barnette's grandfather had taught her and her mother the value of investing. When Barnette inherited her mother's AT&T shares and her parents' house, she became a major investor. She began funneling money into an IRA and a mutual fund. She knows a good thing when she sees it. "I had some friends who had attended Harvard Busi-

> **A WEALTHY VISION:** As opposed to the big picture macro view, a Wealthy Vision encourages you to look inward and identify your comparative advantage—your unique gifts based upon a blend of innate characteristics.

ness School and they told me to invest in the T. Rowe Price Mutual Fund. I still own that fund today." Barnette had developed a Wealthy System.

> Successful people set up a **WEALTHY SYSTEM** that allows them to remain organized. This is the habit that allows them to track resources, manage their finances, and adopt money management and investment processes that allow them to monitor their progress.

To continue learning about money, Barnette became a certified financial planner. This made her an even better investor, and she reads *The New York Times* and *Barron's* regularly. Developing the habit of acquiring knowledge has helped her become a more competent and confident investor. When it comes to learning, Barnette can never get enough.

A WEALTHY APPETITE is nurtured by acquiring knowledge. To add value, wealthy women continually increase their knowledge base. They gain insight by attending seminars, subscribing to periodicals, and reading books to stay abreast of the economy and to identify investment opportunities.

During a brief recession in the nineties, Barnette was faced with adversity, and although some brokers turned their attention to other interests, she forged ahead and recovered eventually. She had demonstrated the attribute of a Wealthy Mindset.

A WEALTHY MINDSET keeps you going in the face of adversity. Everyone else might tell you something is impossible, but a Wealthy Mindset keeps you moving to the beat of your own drum.

Barnette continues working in real estate, but keeps an eye out for good investments. She says of her stocks, "I rarely sell unless it's a loss being used to offset a gain. I buy solid companies and invest for the long term. The market and the economy are cyclical and if you invest you will prosper eventually. You must be diversified and you must have cash and you need to have fixed-income investments." Barnette declined to share the size of her portfolio. She did say that she feels certain that her mother would be very proud of her.

A WEALTHY LEGACY is about investing in others. This habit promotes the importance of paying your way forward. To receive, you must first give something of value. People who develop this habit recognize that it is in giving that they receive, and they relish the opportunity to leave a path for others to follow.

Barnette might never have shared her story, and believe me when I say it took a bit of coaxing on my part. She relented because she was convinced that others might benefit from her gains. If only one reader is able to stay the course because she has read Barnette's story, her success will demonstrate the power of a Wealthy Legacy.

. . . .

Now that you have been reintroduced to the Wealthy Habits, it's time to think, act, and become a wealthy women. The stories I've presented in *Purse* focus on women who were determined to become financially independent:

- to control their money instead of letting money control them.
- to provide for their future by themselves.
- to learn what they need to know.
- to make choices that move toward their goal.

HOW THE WEALTHY WOMAN THINKS

Claudia married a foreign service officer right after college and did not work outside the home initially. "You couldn't work overseas if you were married to an officer. I had worked during college and I knew a woman needed her own money." Eventually Claudia sold real estate part time, and after her divorce she built a flourishing business that helped her achieve financial independence. "When it comes to money don't assume someone is going to take care of you and don't be taken advantage of. You cannot depend on your husband's largesse."

Claudia thinks differently than she did when she first got married. Knowledge and experience have transformed the way she thinks about wealth. The same can be said of all the other wealthy women that we have discussed in *Purse*. Their thinking has changed over time, and they see money, spending, opportunities, and their future in a particular way.

Wealthy women think differently from other women. They view money uniquely and develop patterns of behavior and thought that keep them in front financially. Now that you see how wealthy women think, you can compare it to your own way of thinking and make any adjustments that you want.

ABOUT MONEY

Wealthy women like Claudia think differently about money from their counterparts. They think of money as a tool to help them achieve what they want. Like a key, money is a tool that can be used to unlock doors, important doors that determine the way a person lives today and in the future. Wealthy women realize money is the tool that can help them to become financially independent and help fund their philanthropic endeavors.

When wealthy women look at their money, they generally ask themselves, "What's the best use of this money?" They weigh the answer carefully. They understand that every decision has consequences, and they look ahead to see what those consequences might be. Claudia's choices about money were driven by her goal of financial independence. She knows, as wealthy women do, that once the money is spent on, say, a blouse, it's gone. They can't use it anymore. They aren't opposed to buying blouses, but they are opposed to buying blouses thoughtlessly. They know that the money for one blouse could be invested and grow to become enough to buy ten blouses in a few years.

Wealthy women also ask themselves, "How can I make this money make more money?" They're experts at putting their money to work—employing it, so to speak, to create more. When money makes money, goals are achieved. That's how wealthy women think about money.

I also notice that wealthy women associate money with freedom. Money buys choices over one's life. Too often a lack of money keeps women in bondage to a life they don't want. Investors like the freedom that money gives them, and they keep their money making more money so that they can maintain that freedom.

How does this compare to the way you think about money? If you think about money like a wealthy woman, you will see it as the tool that can create the life you want. If you work, you trade time for money. When you have enough money working for you, you can quit. You have a choice about whether you trade time for money. That is what true financial freedom is.

ABOUT SPENDING

Wealthy women spend their money on making more money before they spend it on things that won't make them money. Claudia had a Wealthy Vision for herself, so her first money each month is spent investing in that dream. She has a plan and sticks to it. She pays herself first, and then she pays her bills. She enjoys spending what's left on her life right now.

Wealthy women adopt the habit of a focus, allowing their goals to drive their spending. They look at a $2,400 Chanel handbag and know that it could buy a hundred shares of a utility stock they've been watching. They may buy the purse, but it's a careful choice, not a thoughtless one. It would cut into money they are spending on their future, and they think that the trade-off is worth it.

Wealthy women resist instant gratification, and you won't hear many of them rationalizing about why they just *had* to buy that new sofa. They are independent in their thinking about money and aren't swayed by what others do or buy.

For wealthy women, spending is intentional and always in-line with their plan. This is why wealthy women adopt systems that assist them with staying aligned with their future. For them, this is the way to be sure that they will retain tomorrow the same life and freedom of choice they enjoy today.

How does this compare with the way you think about spending? If you think about spending like a wealthy woman, you will see it as something that you do to support; not sabotage, your life plan.

ABOUT OPPORTUNITIES

Wealthy women are continually confronted with opportunities. The wealthy women in *Purse* utilize several of the wealthy behaviors to help them filter opportunities:

- They resist invading their existing investments or their savings at all costs. If seizing an opportunity means taking money from another investment, they probably won't do it.

- They do their homework before deciding whether to pursue an investment opportunity. They research all aspects of the company until they feel confident that it will be a good investment.

- They are decisive, and once they make a decision, they stick with it and don't look back.

- They think about long-term security, not short-term volatility.

- They learn from their mistakes and move on rather than vow never to invest again.

- They know that opportunities come and go; if they don't catch this one, another will come along. They are patient.

- They are skeptical and tend to go the other way when everyone else is investing in a trendy stock.

How does this compare with your thinking about opportunities? If you think about opportunities like wealthy women, you will see them as choices that are good for you only if they fit your timetable, risk level, and current financial situation.

ABOUT COMPANIES

Wealthy women see businesses as potential investments, not simply places to shop. They pay attention to a company's products, management changes, and signs of expansion.

They also understand balance sheets and can read the financials of a company. They know how to research using the opinions of analysts or research companies. This information is accessible over the Internet and at your local library.

Women are particularly good at spotting companies that might make good investments because women are the world's chief consumers. They know what works and what doesn't. They know what stores offer the best products and services. They know when a product that every mother wants hits the market, and they can tell you the same about what kids want. This puts women at an advantage in selecting companies to invest in.

Peter Lynch, former portfolio manager of Fidelity's Magellan Fund, suggests that you buy what you know. One of his best stock investments was Sara Lee—he purchased the stock because his wife saw women buying pantyhose that were packaged in egg-shaped containers at the supermarket. This is why women are good investors. They can spot a trend happening. How does this compare with your thinking about companies? If you think about companies like a wealthy woman, you will use the Wealthy Mindset and see them as potential money-makers for you.

ABOUT CHOICES

Wealthy women see choices as trade-offs. They understand that the higher the potential risk, the higher the potential reward. Investors always weigh possible outcomes, don't take risks lightly, and have little sense of urgency. They take time on the front end of a choice to save time and money on the back end.

Wealthy women know that when they lose money, they have to make more money to replace it. They try to avoid this unpleasant experience.

How does this compare with your thinking about choices? If you think about choices like a wealthy woman, you will see them as financial moves that can help you or hurt you. You will also understand that for every choice you make, there is a trade-off.

ABOUT RISK

Wealthy women do what they can to minimize risk. They don't want to lose money, because it takes them in the wrong direction.

Reducing risk as an investor means that you will take the following steps:

- Invest in a number of different investment products. That way, if one drops, the others will make up for it. This is called asset allocation. You allocate your assets here and there across the investment spectrum.

- Seek advice from a professional whom you trust and who knows you.

- Continue learning so that you can spot bad advice when you hear it.

- Stay true to your instincts.

- Remember, risk exists whether you put your money in the bank, in the stock market, or under the mattress.

Having said that, I want you to know that wealthy women expect to lose money, no matter how hard they try to avoid it. They've learned that not all stocks or funds will perform well even when it appeared that they would. Loss is inevitable, but the success of the market over time supports investing. I've seen some investors lose money and never return to the market. Unfortunately, they've let their fear keep them from recovering and moving forward. Don't mistake volatility for risk. Volatility is the ups and downs of the market.

How does this compare with your thinking about risk? If you think like a wealthy woman about risk, you will take precautions, understand that some loss is inevitable, and stick with your plan.

ABOUT THE FUTURE

Wealthy women acquire the habit of a Wealthy Outlook and are optimistic about their future. They don't worry because they have prepared for their future. This allows them to spend joyfully today because they have set aside enough for tomorrow.

A sense of control over your future enables you to be flexible about it. For example, you may have a goal of retiring at forty-five and then decide to keep working. If you have the funds set aside, you will have the flexibility to choose.

This speaks to the importance of revisiting your goals once a year to be certain that you still want to do what you planned. Many things happen on the way to your future, and you want to be able to move in new directions if they are a closer fit to the person you have become.

The wealthy woman knows that having a Wealthy Focus and achieving goals are really just answers to the question of how she wants her life to be, and that the important thing is to have enough money to support her choices.

How does this compare with your thinking about the future? If you think about the future like a wealthy woman, you will be optimistic and flexible because you will have already visited the future and deposited money in it.

WHOM THE WEALTHY WOMAN TRUSTS

The wealthy woman trusts herself first. She has developed a Wealthy Appetite and has acquired the knowledge needed to select investment products and advisors. In addition to trusting herself, to help her succeed financially the wealthy woman assembles others to:

Give her advice: The wealthy woman gets her advice from professionals and avoids advice from well-meaning family and friends.

Make her trades: She executes trades through a broker and occasionally on her own. Women increasingly are using online brokerage services and research tools, but most do this in addition to their work with a broker, not as a replacement.

Manage her earnings/losses: The wealthy woman uses a tax professional, but keeps accurate and organized records herself.

Create her financial plan: She uses a financial planner as her financial quarterback to help oversee her entire financial condition and progress. She is very particular about who this person is and doesn't hesitate to interview several planners before settling on one in particular.

Build her estate: The wealthy women has an estate-planning team, including her financial planner and an estate-planning attorney.

Monitor her progress: She reviews her own progress monthly and at least annually with advisers.

Protect her assets: The wealthy woman protects her assets by having her attorney draw up her will and trust.

Prepare her reports: More and more investors use computer software to track their money and print out reports other than those prepared by accountants and attorneys.

HOW THE WEALTHY WOMAN LEARNS

The wealthy woman has developed the habit of a Wealthy Appetite for information and is a learner. She reads, watches, talks, and takes classes. She creates her own reservoir of information, from subscribing to newspapers such as *The Wall Street Journal* or *The New York Times* to making financial sites such as www.money.com her

Internet home page. She has her favorite financial channel on TV, such as Bloomberg, and tunes in to her favorite show, such as public television's *Nightly Business Report.* As her knowledge grows, so does her ability to screen information that comes to her from advisors, and her skill in making smart decisions.

The wealthy woman knows that financial information is not beyond her ability to understand. She holds her advisors accountable and doesn't pretend that she understands something when she doesn't. She learns that if a professional can't describe a financial concept or product clearly, she may not want to continue the relationship. She attends classes and seminars in her area and beyond. As she advances in her knowledge and activity, she may also choose to attend stockholders' meetings in various parts of the country.

The wealthy woman also likes to stay in step with technology. She may receive stock quotes and portfolio updates on her wireless phone or PDA.

The wealthy woman knows that learning is an essential ingredient to ongoing success. Most enjoy it and find it satisfying to stay on the cutting edge of information about the resources that will fund their future.

How does this compare with the way you think about learning? If you acquire the habit of a Wealthy Appetite, you will see learning as your responsibility to yourself and will increase your future prosperity.

WHAT THE WEALTHY WOMAN DOES

Let's see what the wealthy woman does:

With her earnings: She pays herself first, invests at least 10 percent of her income (often more), participates in employer-sponsored plans, and uses advisors to help her make smart choices about her earnings.

To manage advisors: She schedules appointments as needed with her advisors, and she never misses her annual appointments with them.

To fit investing into her busy life: She adopts Wealthy Systems that utilize automatic investment programs deducted from her payroll and savings accounts, lets a stock information service send her data over the Internet to her wireless device, reads the financial column over coffee in the morning, and meets with other women on the same financial path once a week for lunch.

To manage her fears, the wealthy woman:

- Conveys her concerns to her advisors immediately.
- Faces her fears instead of letting them fester.
- Leaves little or no room for wondering how things are by looking at all statements monthly.
- Listens to sources that are sound, not sensational. For example, when the market goes down a few points, many television reporters say, "The market took a tumble today." But when it goes up a few points, they report "a modest gain." She focuses on her long-term goals and doesn't react to daily commentary.

. . . .

In order to fill your purse and live the wealthy lifestyle, you may need support. In the final chapter I will share how you can use the power of many purses to assist you with this journey. These groups will assist you beyond the financial rewards by providing camaraderie as well as accountability. As you increase your sense of control over yourself and your future you will begin to experience the financial peace of mind that comes with having a full purse strapped over your shoulder.

Striking a Balance

In this chapter, the wealthy woman demonstrated the utilization of a host of feminine/masculine attributes, which include being adaptable, humble, empathic, compassionate, persuasive, spontaneous, receptive, nurturing, intuitive, savvy, verbal, and sensitive. Admirable masculine characteristics include being ambitious, assertive, confident, disciplined, courageous, decisive, organized, analytical, competitive, independent, and rational.

If the spirit moves you, write about these strengths in your life.

_____

_____

_____

_____

_____

_____

_____

_____

_____

_____

TEN | THE SISTERHOOD OF THE PURSE

THE POWER OF PURSES

IN THIS CHAPTER YOU CAN LEARN HOW TO GATHER the support you need by forming a Purse Group. Meeting with friends regularly, you can learn how to live a wealthy lifestyle by adopting the 7 Wealthy Habits. You will learn how to build wealth together and offer one another support as you learn together and handle your investments individually. As you now know, tolerating the volatility of the market is essential for successful investing. And having a Purse Group to soothe your nerves during market tumult is as close as you're going to get to a financial version of healing balm in Gilead. In bringing their individual talents and sensibilities to the table, Purse Group members help one another transform into wealthy women.

Another important purpose of the Purse Group is to support you in your journey to become more knowledgeable about investing and as a source of accountability. I'm sure you may have joined a book club or investment club; it would be helpful to think of Purse Groups as a hybrid. Because you will be using *Purse* as the curriculum, it will be easy for potential members to mischaracterize your Purse Group to a book club. To that end, the one-and-a-half to two-hour time frame should be managed with an eye on keeping members on task.

CHOOSING YOUR MEMBERS

Before contacting friends about forming a Purse Group, you may want to consider which women in your life would bring the most to the table. Of course you're going to want to like one another, because there will be times when you confide your fears and vulnerabilities. But you'll also want to consider who's reliable and can make a commitment to show up on time and be prepared to contribute. Consider also personality styles. Members should be able to work together even if there is some tension.

I have belonged to several investment clubs and have fond memories of our times together. Many women love to socialize and entertain, and the meetings I attended often evolved into great parties and networking events. It got to a point where the hostesses competed to see who could serve the best appetizers and beverages. Purse Ladies, let me say that it's okay to make it a social event, but the main course should be about building wealth and sharing your success along the way. To that end, it is better if you stick to light refreshments such as coffee, soda, tea, and a small dessert or fruit and cheese tray.

Each member will be asked to keep a Purseonal Journal to reflect on the concepts covered and to record their feelings. Remember, this is a support group, and building wealth affects the heart and the head. Purse Groups are action oriented and designed to help members internalize the wealthy principles that are the core foundation of *A Purse of Your Own.*

Aim for limiting your Group to eight to ten women so everyone will have a chance to speak and be heard. It's best to contact people who have similar financial needs. For instance, financially successful women might grow impatient if they have to spend most of their time in the Group consoling someone who is broke because she blows most of her money on new clothes. This is not to say that you should exclude anyone who shows a sincere interest in getting her financial health in order. Let commitment be the strongest quality you seek when attracting members to your Purse Group. You can accomplish great things when the Group is in sync and leveraging one another's strengths.

In forming Purse Groups, you may choose to connect with women friends and acquaintances with a variety of different strengths. For a sampling of strengths, see the Purseonality Quiz in Chapter One of this book, page 8. The quiz was designed to highlight individual strengths, and can be distributed during one of your Purse Group meetings. As a Group, the fusion of your minds and talents can help you create wealth.

EXTENDING INVITATIONS

When you begin contacting friends, relatives, neighbors, or classmates, be clear about the purpose of Purse Groups. You might want to send an invitation such as this one:

Dear _____
I'm reading A Purse of Your Own, *a female-friendly investment guide written by a wealth coach for women who are tired of leading unwealthy lives and want to become financially independent. I'm starting a Purse Group and I'm inviting you*

to join. We will meet regularly to learn how to make money work for us, as opposed to just working for our money. We won't be pooling money, but we can cheer one another on as we get better about managing what we have, and adopting the habits that lead to real wealth and ultimately to financial independence.

Please join me at [name a date, time, and location] to decide on a regular time and a location for meetings. All you need to do is show up on time and bring a copy of A Purse of Your Own *by Deborah Owens with Brenda Lane Richardson. Hope you can make it.*

RSVP by [Date] to _____.

FOR YOUR FIRST MEETING

1. Gather in a circle if possible, so no one feels left out.
2. Ask each participant to take turns introducing herself and explaining in a few sentences what she hopes to get out of the Group.
3. Capture those expectations on a flip chart or legal pad and use this list as a guide for determining which topics and exercises in *Purse* should be emphasized in your upcoming meetings.
4. Agree on a time and place for meeting and, if necessary, explore options for child care.
5. Set up a few ground rules: For instance, a few of you may want to take turns leading the Group. Explain that what gets said in the meeting should be kept confidential, so that

people will feel comfortable expressing their deepest feelings.

6. You might want to set a time limit on individual shares so that no one dominates the discussion. It also helps to set a time limit on meetings, anywhere from one to two hours, and set the frequency (once a month or biweekly).

7. Decide on five to eight expectations that the Group has for itself, such as for each member to start investing by a certain time period, or for each member to start making regular contributions to a mutual fund by a certain date. Expectations may also include how much of *Purse* should be read between group meetings, such as half a chapter or five to ten pages, etc.

8. Settle on a time period for the meetings. For instance, if you agree to continue meeting for a year, some members should feel free at the end of that period to stop attending, while others might want to continue meeting and perhaps introduce a new member to the Group.

9. Ask members to make a pact to continue attending meetings even during difficult times in their lives and when they are going through times of financial turmoil. Members undergoing personal difficulties will leave the meetings feeling a lot better than when they started.

10. Assign roles. The leader might ask someone to volunteer to record important notes, such as plans and details for a scouting trip (to explore investment options) or where the next meeting will be held. Someone else may volunteer to be a timekeeper who signals when the meeting should begin and end, and to keep individual members from taking up

too much time. And finally, women can volunteer to take turns as "readers" by keeping an eye out for relevant articles from magazines or newspapers that can be shared at the meeting. Remember that the 7 Wealthy Habits should be displayed prominently and discussed at each of your sessions, so you might ask someone else to brainstorm about how to use them regularly in your Group.

ONCE YOUR MEETINGS BEGIN

Start with a check-in, when members take turns sharing how they're feeling, any particular challenges that might have come up, and how they feel about their progress in creating a wealthier life— which means adding something of value. Purse Group members give "shares" at the beginning of the meeting in order to create an environment of support and learning. To that end, each member should be prepared to share what she learned in the previous meeting and how she will apply and then internalize one of the Wealthy Habits. The leader should encourage everyone to share and should keep discussions on track.

1. The leader can read aloud the list of Group expectations.
2. Members should take two to three minutes describing their efforts to fulfill the goals they listed at the last meeting. No excuses or long explanations, just a few words needed here.
3. Start a discussion by reading aloud from *Purse,* with members joining in with relevant information. This is also a time to bring up relevant information clipped from financial publications. A few months into your meetings, discuss

the possibility of inviting local financial experts to discuss specific topics, or taking field trips.

4. In the final ten minutes, members can take turns stating aloud goals that they hope to accomplish before the next meeting. The goals should be practical and doable.

5. Some Groups feel comfortable ending with a moment of silence or prayer to give members meditation time, while others begin and end with financial inspirations. These can be quotes from *Purse*.

Here's an example of what an agenda should cover in the first meeting. You can use this as the template for each meeting as you proceed through each chapter.

Agenda

1. Welcome—Read introduction from *Purse*. Review the 7 Wealthy Habits.

2. Shares—What you hope to achieve by joining the Purse Group. (Use a flip chart, white board, or legal pad to record the responses.)

3. Discuss goals and objectives, and record them to review at the end of the meeting.

4. Discuss revelations that came up during Purseonal Journal entries.

5. Create your Purse Group Mission Statement.

6. Assign homework for the next meeting: Cleaning out your purse; balance sheet.

MOTIVATION AND INCENTIVES

Purse Groups are designed to motivate. Create rewards and incentives for members as they achieve their goals. Each member can contribute something as little as $5 a week into a purse, and this money can be rewarded to members who have achieved a Purseonal goal like paying off a credit card or funding an IRA. Or you can let the contributions build up and one member can qualify to win the contents. Once the purse is emptied another member can qualify to earn the contents, provided it is used toward achieving a wealthy goal.

Continue to use your creativity in your Purse Group by integrating the Wealthy Habits into the culture of your meetings. This is how you support the members and create an environment that empowers your Purse Sisters on their path to a wealthy lifestyle.

SUPPORT ADDS VALUE

Support can be an important part of your wealth-building success. Weight Watchers conducted a study of women trying to lose weight, and found that getting support accompanied an improvement in the participants' ability to control their eating and choose lower-calorie foods. The same holds true with improving your Purseonal balance sheets. Members who join may have goals that can be pretty daunting if they are novices. Your weekly discussion topics, along with members sharing their challenges and triumphs, can help them acquire the habit of a Wealthy Focus, which will allow them to stay the course in the face of adversity.

THE POWER OF AFFIRMATION

Create an e-mail list to streamline the communication tasks and as a means of sharing the success and achievements of the members. Wealthy women recognize that the secret to achieving goals is accountability. Purse Groups can be really effective when members share their financial goals and chart their progress monthly at the meetings. Using the needs and goals exercise in Chapter One is an excellent way to identify Purseonal goals, the beginning steps to creating a Wealthy System. Your Purse Group can provide the resolve that members may seek to break unwealthy habits. As members share and affirm their success in achieving their financial goals they will transform.

KEEPING IT FRESH

One of the ways you can add variety to your Purse Group is to host field trips and have meetings at different locations. Encourage members to share information about seminars that can assist them in acquiring more knowledge about the financial markets and investing. National financial conferences are hosted at local convention centers and at business schools on college campuses; these can make for fun group outings. Encourage members to bring relevant articles from magazines and newspapers, with an eye on sparking discussion and boosting the groups' Purseonality Quotient (PQ). Learning to understand the language of finance and investing, coupled with current events, helps women be less intimidated by the financial markets and ultimately builds confidence. Sharing information with one another further facilitates Group dynamics.

AVOIDING PITFALLS

The success of your Purse Group depends on the engagement of your membership. The greatest threat to your Purse Group is lack of clear expectations and commitment from the members. In one of the Groups that I coached, the majority of the members were extremely busy and less than half attended the meetings regularly. Although they were initially highly motivated, their interest dwindled. In my opinion, the Group failed because they did not complete the required reading or homework assignments, and as a result, the meetings were disorganized and members were not engaged. The aim of the Group should be to keep each Purse Sister coming back for more. Everyone should feel she can't afford to miss a meeting.

Strong and cohesive Groups can be achieved if all members participate in the preparation of the activities. Your Group is the support system designed to help your Purse Sisters internalize the Wealthy Habits that are shared in *Purse*. Remember to spread the wealth by rotating roles and responsibilities each month. This prevents burnout and resentment that can render the Group ineffective. Purse Groups should be interactive and foster participation by all the members in order to create a desire for attendance.

GROUP PURSERCISES:
INTERNALIZING THE HABITS

Purse has a number of insightful exercises that can assist your Group with incorporating the Wealthy Habits into their life styles.

A Getting-to-Know-You Themed Share

Ask members to read this aloud at the first meeting so that they can follow up at the next meeting by sharing their own Purse Stories.

Your ability to handle money is largely dependent on emotional factors that you can't afford to ignore. So take this opportunity to share your Purse Stories: emotional/financial histories. Psychologists have long known that we operate according to a narrative comprised of real facts, perceptions, and unconscious beliefs. If a story suggests, for instance, that no matter what you do, you'll never get ahead, you will find it almost impossible to succeed. So it's important for you to uncover the unconscious script, and if necessary, rewrite it.

You'll be able to identify your Purse Story because it will have revealed itself in a pattern throughout your life. Maybe you can never stick to a budget, or you are always careening from one financial drama to another. This is the kind of work that requires you to get real with yourself and follow the path back through your past to examine events that may have led you in this direction. You may also want to start listening to the way you put yourself down. Perhaps you describe yourself as lazy or as a procrastinator. You might use phrases like "always a day late and a dollar short." In listening to yourself, you will want to search through your early experiences for events that may have convinced you that you cannot succeed financially.

One woman, Leslie, 42, was reminded of her Purse Story when she described an antique purse that her mother had purchased during the fifties. "It's a pearly gray Lucite with a hard, glossy finish. That may not sound great, but it was elegant then and still is. When I use it, people stop me and ask about it. I could sell it for at least a thousand dollars, but I never would. Seeing it, I picture my mom as a young, forceful woman. She bought that purse when she was feeling flush with cash, decades after moving to New York.

"She was a farmer's daughter, and was expected to remain in Virginia and marry a local man. But she moved to New York, found work, and when my father abandoned her, leaving her with two babies, she refused to accept public assistance. She took my sister and me to Virginia, left us with her sister, and went back to New York to earn money. I was just eight months old."

Leslie and her sister were separated from their mother for three years, an extraordinarily long time for a child. Through office work, real estate investment, and starting a series of businesses, her mother was able to create wealth. In fact, Leslie grew up in an eleven-room house in a fashionable New York neighborhood. You would think that this rich inheritance would give Leslie the start she needed to create wealth of her own, but that wasn't the case.

Leslie spent the first several decades of her life overspending on fancy clothes and shoes. She now realizes that she was deeply affected by her mother's abandonment. "I was secretly convinced I was worthless, why else would my mother have chosen to leave me? On a rational level, I was proud of her for being so determined, but I was hurt. It's very difficult to admit that our parents caused us harm. But I've learned to look at it like this: If someone steps on your foot, it may be an accident, but that doesn't mean you aren't hurt. If you think of yourself as unworthy, and you don't recognize that you can make hurtful decisions like buying clothes that you can't afford, or taking expensive vacations to cheer yourself up, even though the truth is that spending is only going to make you more depressed."

Her mother died in 1987. After working through grief and her abandonment issues, Leslie found the gray purse at the back of a shelf. "I consider it one of my most important gifts from my mother. It's a reminder that I am worthy and valuable, and that I want to continue adding to that value. I've filled her purse with copies of my financial documents as a symbol of my power in this world. When I changed the way I viewed myself, my financial life changed."

Now you can share or write your own Purse Stories. What family history is influencing your financial decisions? Write the details in your Purse Journal and share them with other members. If it's a damaging story (you'll know that it is if you're unhappy with your finances), rewrite it and share the details about where you're going and what you hope to do.

An At-Home Pursercise That Members Can Discuss Together

Label an old purse "Wealth," another "Loss." To Loss, add credit card receipts and anything representing money that's gone for good. To Wealth, add photocopies of receipts that represent adding to your value (tuition, CD accounts, mortgage payments). Review the contents regularly, until your Wealth bulges. After six months report on what your purses reveal.

An Out-and-About Pursercise

Encourage Purse Group members to always keep an eye out for good investments. When visiting a favorite restaurant chain or retailer—shopping for pharmaceuticals, toys, office supplies, groceries, etc.—if an opportunity arises, ask an employee how the business is doing. Keep an eye out for established businesses going through hard times, so you can buy low. When you discover something interesting, share what you learned with other Purse Group members.

Suggested Exercises That Work Well with a Group:

The Comparative Advantage exercise on page 54
The Purse Diary on page 230
The Purse scrapbooking on page 174
Building an imaginary portfolio on page 89 (when you've finished, compare performances)

For more Pursercises and resources, refer to the Pursessentials starting on page 213. Remember that the more creative you are, the more successful your Purse Group will be.

PAYING IT FORWARD

Purse Sisters, have fun with your Group and please make it inclusive. Don't be afraid to invite other ladies into your Group as you progress. If you believe bringing someone new into the Group would be disruptive because of the Group dynamics, pay it forward and encourage this person to start her own Purse Group. Allow her to visit one of your meetings and share some of your insights with her. Spawning other Purse Groups demonstrates a Wealthy Legacy.

I hope you will continue to pay it forward by adding more exercises to the purse community at www.deborahowens.com. Send us Group pictures and share your stories on the purse community bulletin board in order to encourage others. You can learn about live Purse of Your Own Events and have access to additional ideas and resources by signing up as a Purse Sister at the website.

In the meantime, may the purse be with you.

PURSESSENTIALS

· · · · · · · · ·

Like that tube of ChapStick or the emery board that you keep in your purse, Pursessentials are tools and resources designed to fit specific circumstances. Whether it's addressing your credit score or hiring a financial advisor, you can find the solutions that allow you to put the finishing touches on your finances.

PURSESSENTIAL # 1: CUTTING BACK ON EVERYDAY EXPENSES

The following ideas will help you ensure that you have money to invest.

Save on Food and Beverages

- Look for two-for-one or "early bird" specials if you eat in restaurants with friends who are also trying to save more money.
- Cook on weekends, and use the frozen dinners the rest of the week.
- Order from the children's menu when you go out to eat.

Save on Commuting

- Keep your car on its scheduled maintenance so that it will last longer.
- Wash your own car and pump your own gas.
- Some gas stations even give free or discounted car washes with gas purchases.

Save on Your Telephone

- Do you really need a home phone? If so, don't pay for an expensive plan. Many people now are using their cell phones as their main and/or only phone line.
- Make free long-distance calls over the Internet by downloading software from www.Skype.com.
- Look at your phone bill. Do you really need the extra line, caller ID, call waiting, and call forwarding?

Save on Clothing

- Look through your closet with new eyes. Allow yourself to feel gratitude for the clothing and accessories that you have acquired.
- Demonstrate your appreciation by wearing what you have and encouraging yourself to enjoy the experience.
- Declare a moratorium on shopping, lasting from two months to a year, depending on your financial needs.
- Find a fashionable consignment shop where you can sell some of the clothes that you no longer wear, and if you truly need something, shop while you're there.
- Swap clothes with a friend.

Save on Entertainment

- Reassess your cable TV costs. If you need it only for reception, get the basic plan.
- Cut out cable and download missed episodes of favorite shows from network sites; try www.hulu.com or www.nbc.com.

- Share rental movies with friends or check out DVDs from the library.
- Go to matinees to see new films.
- Ask for senior discounts if you're old enough. You'd be surprised at how often you get them.

Save on Insurance

- Check your insurance premiums. Get quotes online (www .Quotes.com) or from an insurance broker or agent to see if you can save some money on your premiums.
- You may get a better rate by having your home or renter's insurance with the same carrier as your auto insurance.

Save on Miscellaneous Items

- Walk or ride your bike instead of joining a gym or paying a personal trainer. If you don't have a bike, buy a used one at a flea market or on www.craigslist.com.
- Instead of buying lottery tickets, put the money into your interest-bearing cash reserve account. Your odds of winning are better.
- Clean your own house.
- Mow your own lawn. It's good for your mind, your body, and your pocketbook.
- Shop for Christmas all year long and take advantage of sales.
- Get a roommate or rent a room in your home. If you rent to a student who won't be there all year long, you'll still have some privacy.

- Save money in an interest-bearing account for big items such as furniture, and buy when you have the money instead of financing on credit.
- Research large items that you plan to buy on the Internet to save gas and time, and avoid falling for persuasive salespeople.
- Take enough cash from each paycheck to get you through that period, and avoid two stops at the ATM. Keep track of where that cash is going.

If you've investing $10,000 or more, you might want to consult with an advisor. The vast number of products and investment vehicles and the incredible array of mutual funds, stocks, bonds, and other investments can cause a bad case of analysis paralysis. An advisor can help you navigate through unfamiliar territory.

If you do decide to work with a financial advisor, it's important to remember that *you* are doing the hiring, not the other way around.

The bottom line on selecting an advisor is that you should do homework. There is no substitute for preparation, and because the individual you select may work with you for some time, you should do as much preparing and interviewing as needed until you find the right fit for your situation.

First, decide what you want from a financial advisor. Here are four important goals:

- Create and grow wealth for you.
- Protect and preserve your wealth.
- Plan for the most tax-advantaged distribution of wealth during life.
- Plan for the most tax-advantaged distribution of wealth at death.

QUALITIES OF AN EFFECTIVE ADVISOR

It is essential that a good advisor be:

TRUSTWORTHY

Since your financial journey will last a lifetime, be certain that you trust the advisor(s) you're bringing with you on the trip. Trustworthiness is first because it is the foundation for your relationship. All the good looks, smooth talk, and letters after her last name on her business card don't mean much if you don't have faith in what she's telling you. Having trust and faith means having a comfortable feeling about the path you're on; not having it means questioning almost everything that your advisor recommends and hating her during market turmoil.

AN EDUCATOR

A good advisor must be an educator. Most people who are good at their profession possess this trait. A good teacher communicates well and is willing to explain something more than once and in more than one way, if necessary. Remember, advisors have gone to school to learn what they know. Expect an advisor to translate terms and concepts to you in ways that you can grasp, and never be afraid to ask a question more than once.

A good financial advisor will also help you understand whatever investments you may already own, especially those investments that may have been made for you on behalf of your work-related funds. An advisor who educates you will lead you to your best solutions.

A GOOD LISTENER

Have you ever sought advice from someone who did nothing but talk? The expert told you what she thought and gave her opinion, with very little input from you. Frustrating! Advisors must also have the ability to listen if they're going to comprehend your needs and give you insightful advice. You must be able to fully express your goals, fears, hopes, dreams, and present financial situation. Your advisor should listen, take notes, ask questions, and then give you feedback on what you just said. Only then can your advisor start to fully understand where you are now and where you want to go, and then formulate a plan to get you there.

A STRONG COMMUNICATOR

An effective advisor not only listens, but also gives feedback, offering insight and clarity. An advisor in any field must translate language and concepts to the client. A good communicator will make sure that the person listening has a working knowledge of the subject so that the best possible decisions can be made. If she does a good job of communicating her thoughts, you may decide to take her advice. If you don't agree, talk about it until you or she has a different understanding.

OBJECTIVE

Objectivity is crucial in choosing investments. Just because a certain stock or mutual fund has performed well and is the "hot pick" of the moment doesn't mean that it's right for you. A good financial advisor keeps current on new financial products and updated on products already being sold, viewing them objectively with you in mind.

A good financial advisor also doesn't let the amount of commissions paid to her influence her suggestions about what investments will ultimately be chosen for your portfolio. Some advisors maintain relationships with a few funds and plug their clients into one of these favorites. Sometimes that's like trying to stick a square peg into a round hole . . . it's just not a good fit. When interviewing financial advisors, make sure to ask what products they normally choose for their clients. If you can count on one hand the number of mutual funds or stocks mentioned, it's probably a sign that the advisor is too restrictive in her selections.

COMPETENT

Competence may seem like an obvious qualification to you, but it's not always obvious that an advisor is incompetent. Just because someone says she's been a financial advisor for a period of years doesn't mean that she knows what she should know and can do her job at a high level. Professional designations provide you with the assurance that your advisor adheres to certain standards. On the other hand, a professional designation does not guarantee competency nor allow you to disregard your judgment in considering all of the advisor's qualities.

UNDERSTANDING PROFESSIONAL DESIGNATIONS

Let's talk for a minute about the "alphabet soup" of professional designations for financial professionals. Numerous sets of letters can follow a person's name on her business card; each represents a certain area or level of expertise. The following list will help you identify each one and know its meaning.

RR: This advisor is a registered representative with a brokerage house and has passed tests given by the Financial Industry Regulatory Authority, or FINRA. FINRA was created in 2007 to consolidate the National Association of Securities Dealers and the New York Stock Exchange regulatory functions. In order to obtain the license required to sell securities to investors, advisors must take an exam. The most basic license type limits the advisor to the sale of mutual funds and variable annuity and variable life insurance products. The Series 7 license allows your advisor to sell all types of securities: corporate, municipal, options, and variable annuities.

RIA: A registered investment adviser has passed the Series 65 test and the state test where she does business. An RIA may or may not be licensed to sell investments. Usually, an RIA creates financial plans to suit the purpose of the client. RIAs may create plans that include college costs, future retirement income needs, and elder care planning for the client or the client's family.

CFP: Certified financial planners must complete a difficult two-year course during which they are trained in insurance needs, investments, estate planning, and many other facets of investment planning. CFPs not only are able to create financial plans but, if they are licensed, they also may suggest and execute the trades necessary to buy and sell investments for their clients.

CPA: Someone who possesses this designation is a certified public accountant and is thoroughly educated and trained in all areas of taxation. You may hire a CPA each year to prepare your income taxes. CPAs also know about other tax areas including taxes for small businesses, estate taxes, and capital gains taxes.

CLU: Life insurance is always a part of any financial plan, and the certified life underwriter knows how to plan for unexpected emergencies and use life insurance to protect assets. Many people think of life insurance as a policy that pays a certain amount of money when someone dies. But the many uses of life insurance go far beyond that. CLUs can suggest ways to use insurance to reduce income taxes while investing for your child's college education or your retirement, and to eliminate or reduce estate taxes that your heirs will pay after your death.

PFA: A personal financial adviser is a financial planner who has at least five years of experience in the financial planning field and has passed a series of examinations. This is a designation that was created by the National Association of Securities Dealers.

....

A financial designation doesn't guarantee that a particular advisor will be the right one for you. It does mean that an advisor has additional education and expertise beyond what is required to simply create a financial plan or sell investments. It's also a good indication that an advisor has invested much time and effort in being knowledgeable and is dedicated to remaining in the financial services field.

HOW TO FIND AN ADVISOR

The most common way to find an expert, whether it be a plumber, a lawyer, a carpenter, or a financial advisor, is to ask people whom they use and whether they're pleased with the expert's knowledge and service.

If a friend or relative is happy with the service she has received, chances are good that you'll have the same positive experience. But remember that working with a financial advisor for years is different from working with someone on an occasional basis. The commitment to having a good working relationship is much greater.

A great source of information about a professional is another professional. If a CPA prepares your taxes, or if you have a family lawyer or insurance agent, or if you have gotten to know someone at your local bank, ask whom they recommend as a financial advisor. Many times professionals work with one another on an ongoing basis and get to know one another very well. Also, don't be surprised if you ask your CPA, attorney, insurance agent, or bank manager for a referral and that person suggests her own personal financial advisor. It's all about establishing long-term relationships with people you can trust.

Most professionals belong to professional associations or organizations. The Financial Planning Association (FPA) is one that many certified financial planners join. Organizations such as the FPA maintain current rosters of members and may give referrals to the general public. They also offer financial advisors continuing education on new products and developments in their field. The phone number for the FPA is (800) 282-7526; its website is www.fpanet.org.

UNDERSTANDING HOW ADVISORS GET PAID

Just as you wouldn't buy a car without asking how much it costs, you shouldn't select a financial advisor without asking what she charges and how she gets paid. Financial advisors perform a service for which they deserve to be compensated; it's just that compensation can come in many different ways and combinations.

Some financial professionals will give a prospective client a fact sheet that contains information including where they graduated from college, what professional licenses they have, any specialized training courses they've taken, and the fees or commissions they charge. If the financial advisor doesn't offer this information when you interview her, ask for it. Many times the company that the advisor works for will already have a brochure or package with information about the company and how their advisors are compensated. If information about how the advisor is paid is not included in such information, ask to see the contract or application that you must complete to become a client. Information about fees, commissions, and charges must be disclosed to you before you sign a contract to become a client. Make sure you get it.

Discussed in the next sections are some ways that advisors get paid. Remember that many times advisors can receive a combination of these methods.

SALARY

Most financial advisors receive some portion of their pay from a salary, a set amount that they receive every pay period. Imagine a pyramid, with salary being the bottom or base of the pyramid, and fees and commissions layered above it. The base salary for advisors at most brokerage houses is modest.

COMMISSION

A commission is money paid to a salesperson based on the value of the item sold. If an advisor sells stock worth $100 and receives a

1 percent commission, the adviser gets paid $1. You pay a commission every time you buy or sell a stock. Usually, the brokerage house or business where the investment advisor works has a commission schedule based on the number of shares that are sold. Be aware that you may pay more if you buy a smaller-than-usual number of shares of a stock or mutual fund. If you buy one share of a stock, the commission may be just as much or greater than if you buy 100 shares.

Your adviser may be paid what are called "trailing commissions." If you set up a "wealth builder" account, which is done by having a certain amount of your paycheck invested each month, your advisor will also be paid every time new money is invested in your account.

Another member of your advisory team, your insurance agent, is usually paid on commission: a percentage of the policy premiums that are paid during the year.

FEE-ONLY

In the past ten years, a large number of financial advisors have started charging a fee and don't get paid from commissions. A fee-only planner will meet with you, collect information and statements on your present financial situation, find out your goals and plans for the future, and create a financial plan especially for you. It may be a plan for sending your child to college, or it may be more complex with not only college, but also a cruise around the world, retirement planning, elder care planning for you and your spouse, and funding an estate.

Some advisors charge hourly fees ranging from $75 to $500 per hour. Others have standard fees, depending upon the type of plan you need. For example, a plan for funding your child's college education may be $250, and a plan that includes college and retirement may be $500.

ASSET MANAGEMENT FEES

Financial advisors who manage accounts are called "asset managers" and are paid a percentage of tool assets under management. The percentage charged varies by how much your account is worth. Fees can start at 5 percent and decrease to less than 1 percent as the size of your account increases. For example, an account that contains $5,000 may be charged 3 percent, or $150 per year. An account valued at $1,000,000 may be charged .50 percent per year, or $5,000. Certainly, $5,000 is a lot of money, but if you have a good advisor and your account grows $100,000 per year, then paying $5,000 to make $100,000 is a pretty good return.

The old saying "You get what you pay for" is usually true with financial advisors, too. Don't make inexpensive money management fees the primary reason for choosing your investment advisor.

INTERVIEWING AN ADVISOR

You may not have had the experience of hiring someone before. Meeting with and choosing a prospective advisor is not something that should be done quickly or without preparation. During the interview, you may get a gut reaction about the person you're talking with, and I hope you will pay attention to it. But you also shouldn't jump to conclusions or make on-the-spot decisions. Ask the same questions of everyone you meet with, take notes, and then carefully make your choice.

Always interview at least three people for each type of advisor you need. This is a good rule that should not be broken. Why? Because you will learn from each person you talk with, even though you're asking the same questions. Also, each advisor you interview may be from a different company and have different methods of creating plans and ways of getting paid for their services. You can always interview more than three, but you should never interview less.

SAMPLE ADVISOR INTERVIEW QUESTIONS

Before the interview, write down a list of questions that you want your prospective advisor to answer. The following list includes sample questions that you can add to your own:

What is your educational background? Most advisors have college degrees, and some have a master of business administration (MBA) degree, but don't be too impressed by this. It's true, though, that if someone has a master's degree, that person has learned more specialized information than someone with a bachelor's degree. Of course, the degree should be in the area of business and finance and other credentials should be considered.

What are your credentials? In other words, what has this advisor accomplished? Has this person attended advanced financial courses to expand her job knowledge? Has she written and published books on her particular area of expertise? Has she been voted one of the ten best planners in the city? Did someone you trust refer you to her? What designations do you hold? Ideally they will hold one or more of the following: CPA, CFP, or CLU.

What is your background and experience? How long have you been an advisor? Have you worked continuously for the same firm? Do you have a working knowledge of a broad range of investment products, or have you specialized in one particular investment such as bonds? This will give you an indication of their experience and areas of expertise.

What type of clients do you advise? An advisor may have limited the business to only commercial clients with 401(k) plans. Also, some advisors take on only "high-end" clients with $500,000 or more of assets in their accounts.

What type of financial plans do you create? Are the plans for one particular event, such as retirement, or do you create plans that include saving for life events, such as college and retirement? How many pages and illustrations do your plans usually contain? Your goal is to have a thorough, concise plan. A large, elaborate plan with 100 pages may be a lot of fluff. Make sure that you get and pay for only what you really need.

How often do you meet with clients? It's important for you to know how often the advisor reviews client accounts. Many advisors review their clients' accounts daily just to see how certain investments are performing. They don't change investments; they just keep an eye on things. Periodic meetings with clients keep an advisor informed of any events in the client's life, such as the birth of a child, that may affect how a portfolio is invested. Periodic meetings also keep you, the client, educated on how your account is growing and keep you involved in the wealth-building process. Ideally you will want to meet semiannually and annually when you receive your statements.

How are you compensated? The discussion earlier in this chapter will give you a good basis for understanding how an advisor may get paid. You must decide whether you want a fee-only advisor who will create your plan but let you make the investments, or whether you want someone to "tend your garden" and have an active involvement in building your wealth.

Do you have any current clients that I could talk to? This goes back to referrals. Talking with current clients is a great way of finding out how an advisor does the job. You can even ask an advisor's current client some of the questions that were just discussed. Usually, happy customers are willing to let others know about the great service they receive. A current client could be your most valuable source.

....

If you're ready to look for an advisor, remember that you are the one doing the hiring and not the other way around, so you get to decide according to your own criteria. Let this be a confidence-building experience and one that keeps you in the driver's seat.

The secret to any successful diet is that you're much more likely to follow it if you feel motivated, so figure out why you want to start tracking your money in a Purse Diary. As an example, your reasons might include:

I want to:

- find money to invest.
- increase the amount I invest.
- invest in _____ [fill in the name of a particular company or venture].
- start my own business.
- prepare for retirement.
- clean out my purse.
- put together an emergency nest egg.
- invest for [fill in your child's name, or perhaps your own] education.
- get my financial act together, and this is the first step.
- save for a down payment on a home.

If you're collecting receipts and noting your expenditures in your Purse Diary, after you have recorded a week's worth of entries, you can start breaking down expenses in categories. Following are a list of some categories you might include. Please add your own.

- After-school activities
- Allowance
- Bank fees
- Books and periodicals
- Cable TV
- Car (gas, tolls, repairs, etc.)
- Charitable donations
- Child care
- Cigarettes
- Clothes
- Credit cards/loan
- Dentist
- Eating out
- Educational expenses
- Entertainment
- Food (groceries)
- Furniture
- Hair care
- Health care
- Housing (rent, mortgage, repairs, etc.)
- Internet services
- Insurance
- Laundry/dry cleaning
- Liquor, wine, beer
- Mad money fund
- Miscellaneous
- Pet care
- Phone
- Public transportation
- Self-improvement
- Taxes
- Tuition
- Vacation savings

Choose a regular time to track your money so you don't get behind, perhaps during a lunch hour, after a weekend breakfast or dinner on a particular night of the week, or after you get the kids to bed. You get the point. Choose your time and do it. Tracking will give you a sense of control in your life. You don't have to track your spending forever. A few months will give you a feel for it. Once you know it in your bones, you can quit writing things down.

After just a month of tracking, you can begin to focus on what you're learning from your Purse Diary as (1) a way to identify opportunities and (2) to redirect your spending to build wealth.

Debt can diminish your Wealthy Vision and distract you from your goal of building investment wealth. Here are some tips for paying off debts and getting your purse in order.

Take due dates seriously: Pay debts on time and don't give companies a chance to charge you late fees, which is to their financial advantage. Some people mail checks weeks in advance, assuming the money is recorded for the next payment. But that amount may be applied to the previous month. If you're weeks early, call and explain how the money is to be applied. If you're going to be late, call and explain. A supervisor may give you an extra few days without charging a late fee or bumping up your interest rate.

Stop charging but don't cancel: You don't want to cancel all your credit cards at the same time because it will negatively affect your credit score. Besides, longtime membership with a company can boost your score. If you have a spotty repayment record, start paying it off regularly as opposed to one lump sum. If you can't break the charging habit, put your credit cards in a sealed plastic bag that you freeze inside a block of ice. You can thaw out a card if you need it for an emergency.

Resist instant credit card promotions: They seem easy. You're shopping at a store and the clerk says that if you sign up for a card, your bill will be discounted. Every time you apply for a new credit card, activity is reported on your credit report. When there's a flurry of inquiries on your credit report, it works to your disfavor and may make it appear that you are desperately seeking credit.

Tear up blank checks mailed by credit card companies: The aim is to hook you at a desperate time. You may need the cash but you certainly don't need the high interest rate that you will be charged for depositing it into your account.

Go to the top for an interest rate reduction: Once you have a good credit record, phone your credit card customer service department and ask a supervisor to lower your interest rate. If your request is denied, get the name of the company president and the corporate office phone number, and phone that person. When you phone, you will probably be transferred to a high-ranking customer executive, at which point you can continue to lobby for a better rate.

Don't allow an identity thief to snatch your purse: I heard of one case recently in which an identity thief was apprehended, and he showed up in court boldly protesting that *he* was the victim. This thief made such a good case for his lie that the case was postponed and my friend's brother had to spend hundreds in

legal fees before he could prove that he was who he said he was.
Here's what you can do to protect your identity:

- Rather than signing your name on the back of your credit
  cards, write the words: "Ask for ID."
- Keep your Social Security number confidential. If you're
  applying for a job in a place where it might be loosely
  guarded, say that you'll provide this information if you
  become a candidate.
- If you're paying for a purchase online, use a credit card
  that is not connected to your checking account, so thieves
  can't clean it out. Order online only from established
  merchants.
- Keep photocopies of the fronts and backs of credit and
  medical insurance cards in your documents file, so you
  can cancel them right away if necessary.
- Change PIN numbers regularly, and memorize them
  instead of writing them down.
- Keep your mailbox locked and tear up any credit card offers
  or blank checks.
- Don't carry blank checks in your wallet.
- If your purse is stolen, report it immediately and get copies
  of the police report. If you hear from any merchant about
  accounts opened in your name, respond with a notarized
  letter stating that you didn't open the account and attach a
  copy of the police report.
- If your cards are stolen, place a free ninety-day fraud alert
  on your credit file, which signals companies to make a
  double identity check before opening a new account or
  allowing major purchases. You can do this by contacting the

three major reporting agencies: Equifax, (888) 766-0008; Experian, (888) 397-3742; and TransUnion, (800) 680-7289.

A credit freeze is a more drastic response to credit card theft. It allows only the companies that you're already doing business with to gain access to your files and, for the most part, keeps new companies from opening new credit in your name. For more information, go online to www.consumersunion.org/securityfreeze.htm. If you've been avoiding looking at your credit score, now's the time to look at a copy of your credit report.

BOOST YOUR FICO SCORE

Your credit score, also known as a FICO score, was developed by the Fair Isaac Corporation. This three-digit computation ranges from 300 to 850, and serves as a snapshot of your credit history. Consumers with 650 or over are considered good credit risks, and 720 is considered excellent. Companies use this number to gauge your trustworthiness. Credit scores are affected by your history of repaying debt (including long overdue parking and library fines) bankruptcies, bounced checks, foreclosures and liens, court judgments, divorces, and your history with credit card companies.

Your credit score determines how much you have in your purse, because the higher your score, the lower the interest rate you'll be charged on mortgages, apartment and cell phone deposits, credit cards, car loans, and insurance. Just as important, many employers check these scores and the credit reports, and what they learn impacts whether you get hired and what you'll be offered. In May of 2008, the difference on a thirty-year fixed mortgage payment between consumers with the highest and lowest acceptable scores was $1,000 a month.

Three major credit bureaus—Equifax, Experian, and Trans-Union LLC—collect this information and more. You can get a free copy of your annual credit report, which includes your score, by going online to www.annualcreditreport.com or phoning (877) 322-8228. This is the only source for accessing your annual credit report online. The most reliable source of your credit score can be found at www.myFICO.com at a cost of about $50.

To invest, you have to determine whether the company is public, where their shares trade, and if they are available to purchase. You can go online and enter the ticker or full name of a company in a search engine like Google to find the company website, which may include an "Investor" section and the current price of shares. Or you can look for your stock's ticker in the business section of the newspaper or enter the ticker symbol at a website such as www.finance.yahoo.com. Here are directions for working with a broker or going online to buy or sell stocks:

WORKING WITH A BROKER

To buy and sell stocks, bonds, and mutual funds through a brokerage firm, you will need to open a brokerage account. Your stockbroker will ask you to provide your address and Social Security number, and can establish an account immediately. If it is your first trade, you will need to provide a deposit before placing an order. You can transfer funds from your checking or savings account at another institution.

1. You tell your broker to buy 100 shares of ABC Company.
2. Your broker's order department sends the order to their floor clerk on the exchange.
3. The floor clerk alerts a floor trader who then contacts another trader that's willing to sell the 100 shares of ABC. (This is easier than it sounds; floor traders know which floor traders specialize in particular stocks.)
4. The two agree on a price and complete the deal. The notification process goes up the line. Your broker calls back with the final price. The process may take a few minutes, depending on the stock and the market. You will receive a confirmation electronically that confirms how many shares and at what price you purchased.

INVESTING ONLINE THROUGH A BROKER

You can also establish an online account with a financial advisor or stockbroker that allows you to place your own trades and access your accounts online. A lot of wealthy women use professionals for major trades and maintain online accounts for smaller trades.

These are the websites of investment companies that provide advice and support with online access to your accounts:

Fidelity Investments: www.fidelity.com
Schwab Brokerage: www.schwab.com
T. Rowe Price: www.troweprice.com
Scott Trade: www.scotttrade.com

All offer platforms that allow investors to invest in stock and mutual funds from thousands of different investment companies.

Similar to opening an online account, you provide your name, address, and Social Security number and an account can be established immediately.

OPENING AN ONLINE ACCOUNT
ON YOUR OWN

You can invest online with as little as $20 a month; there are a number of online services available. *SmartMoney* magazine conducts an annual survey that compiles rankings of the financial services companies that provide online investing. Visit www.smartmoney.com/ brokers to review a ranking of the top online brokers and learn how they stack up against the competition, and to review their minimum account and transaction fees.

Annual maintenance and transaction fees can impact returns on your investment. So do some comparison shopping, reading the broker fees listed on the websites and keeping an eye out for hidden costs, such as the per-quarter inactivity fees charged by some brokerage companies. The least expensive route is to establish an account with an investment company that does not require a minimum balance or charge an annual fee. You can open an account at www.share builder.com where there's no minimum investment and (in 2008) the transaction fee was $9.95. Many people prefer www.buyandhold .com because it allows them to invest directly in stocks with as little as $20. The Buy and Hold site has a "Buy and Holder IRA" option that eliminates the annual $25 fee if you select the automatic monthly investment option.

ONLINE TRADING

With an online brokerage account you can get almost instant confirmations on trades, and this will give you a sense of control, making you feel one step closer to the market. Once online, the stock trading screen will prompt you with the information required to execute the trade and provide the right instructions.

Indicate that you want to place an order to sell and indicate the number of shares.

Enter the ticker symbol assigned to the company by the exchange it trades on.

You will be prompted to indicate whether your trade is a market or limit order or Good Till Cancelled (GTC). (Remember, a market order is the current price, a limit order means a specific price or better.) All market orders are placed for the day you can place a limit order (GTC).

Even with online investing you are still using a broker to handle your trades; individuals don't have access to the electronic markets. Your online broker accesses the exchange network and the system finds a buyer or seller depending on your order in as short as a few seconds, or in the case of a limit order, it is held by the specialist of the company's stock to be executed if and when the shares reach that price.

Placing a Trade in an Online Brokerage Account

1. You can begin by inputting the number of shares, the ticker symbol, and the price you want to purchase the stock for.

2. If you want the trade executed right away, place a *market order*. You can also place what is called a *limit order* to indicate the specific price for the trade to be executed.

3. Once the trade is executed, the money will be due three days later on a *settlement date*. At that time you will need to transfer funds from your bank account electronically. If this is your first trade the investment company may have required you to deposit funds in advance.

ONLINE SECURITY

Online investing is gaining in popularity, but not everyone is comfortable transacting business online. Many people are still reluctant to have their personal information saved on their computer or stored in a company's database. It's important to have up-to-date security software and a firewall, which protects the information stored on your computer.

Online companies recognize that their customers feel vulnerable in the Internet environment and are responding by making technological innovations that provide security for their customers. The reality is that you take a risk every time you use your credit card at a retailer or restaurant. Making sure your personal information is protected is important online or offline.

To ensure that you're dealing with a reputable company and a secure site, look for affiliations with consumer advocate agencies, such as the Better Business Bureau, and indications that they use encryption technology, which changes the information you enter into an unreadable form and renders it useless to thieves.

A GLOSSARY OF POPULAR
TERMS AND PHRASES

"How about those frontier markets?"

As in days of the Wild West when few people ventured beyond what were considered settled areas, financial pioneers let their investments do the traveling to pre-emerging economies such as Kazakhstan, Kenya, Kuwait, Qatar, and Vietnam, which are a few of the so-called frontier nations. The risk of investing in frontier stocks is that their markets and governments may be functioning shakily, which means you may not be able to liquidate your investments easily or transfer them in a timely fashion, and that can translate into big losses. Seasoned investors may take the risk because frontiers offer opportunities for dramatic gains. This is shaky terrain for novice investors, though.

"Everybody's going for ETFs"

Exchange Traded Funds (ETFs) are like mutual funds in that shareholder money is pooled and invested according to the terms outlined in a prospectus. They hold assets such as stocks or bonds and trade at their net asset value over the course of a trading day, while regular funds are priced once a day, at 4:00 p.m. eastern standard time. ETF's during-the-day-trading feature offers speculative investors an opportunity to bet on the direction of shorter-term market movements. Once considered a novelty, ETFs have risen in popularity. By 2008, there were nearly 800 different choices available, including big cap, small cap, international stocks, emerging markets, energy, technology, real estate, health and financial stocks, and gold bullion. Fees for ETFs are generally low.

"The 52-week high [or low]"

This refers to the highest and lowest price that a stock has traded over the past fifty-two weeks. It helps investors know where the current price fits into the overall recent pattern of a stock's activity. This number changes every day, of course, as today is added and a year ago today is dropped off.

"The last price was 16.50"

This indicates the closing price at which a particular share of stock sold on a given day. A stock does not necessarily open at the same price it closed. If there is news on a company after the market closes, it can create demand that affects the price at which the stock opens the next day.

"It has a small [or medium or large] market cap"

Companies have market caps, or a market value that is calculated by this simple formula: Number of shares times current market price of the shares. In general, the market cap indicates the size and performance of a company. The larger a company is, the less risk there is associated with it. Conversely, the smaller a company is, the lower the market capitalization, and the greater the investment risk. Large caps, also known as blue chips, are considered the most stable. For example, Exxon has one of the largest market capitalizations, at almost $400 billion. This is a direct reflection of the price of the company's stock and the large number of investors who own the available or outstanding shares.

Some companies don't trade on the stock exchange often because they cannot meet the capitalization requirements. Investments in these companies are made over the counter (OTC), where stocks of companies that are "unlisted" trade.

"What was the volume of shares?"

Volume refers either to the total number of shares traded on a given day in all markets, or to the total number of shares traded on a given day by a particular company. Volume indicates the level of activity of a market. A great deal or little activity both generate attention. In 1961, the average daily volume on the NYSE exceeded four million shares; in 2007 it surpassed four *billion* shares in average daily volume, more than 100 times the volume. In the past forty years, the number of individual investors owning mutual funds and the institutional investors purchasing shares have grown significantly, which is reflected in the volume of shares trading on the exchanges.

"I heard [or saw or read] it on Bloomberg"

Bloomberg L.P. is a multimedia company, one of the largest providers of financial information in the world. A Bloomberg terminal provides financial data to investment professionals that they use to analyze companies and provide analysis to their clients. This terminal looks like a computer screen and professionals pay a monthly subscription fee in order to access the data. Bloomberg Television is a financial channel that provides global market commentary and reporting to viewers across the world.

"It's subject to AMT"

The AMT or alternative minimum tax was created to make sure high-net-worth individuals could not escape paying taxes by using creative strategies designed to avoid taxation. Unfortunately, average citizens can trigger the AMT if they exercise stock options or have too much earned income in one year. Always consult with an accountant if you are considering the sale of investments.

"The market bottomed/leveled out"

You'll hear financial commentators discussing the market and using this term. The truth is no one knows whether the market will continue to go down, however, if stocks stop descending lower for consecutive days it is called "bottomed" or "leveled out."

"It's going to split"

When a stock splits, the company is increasing the number of shares outstanding by issuing more to current shareholders. This reduces the price of the shares by half as well. For example, in 2005 Apple stock was trading at $80 a share and the board of directors decided on a two for one split. If you owned 100 shares of Apple (AAPL), you would have received another 100 shares. The stock began trading at $40 a share after the split. (If you'd retained the stock you'd now have 200 shares that traded at $150.00 a share in September of 2008.)

"Capital gains"

Capital gains are what most people think of when they think of stocks. Say that you buy 100 shares of a company for $30 per share. That's a total purchase price of $3,000, not including transaction costs. If the value goes up to $50 per share, your investment is now worth $5,000. If you sell at that point, you would have a capital gain of $2,000 ($5,000 - $3,000 = $2,000). It is important that you keep track of your cost basis—the total amount you originally paid for a stock—so that you can properly report your capital gains for tax purposes.

There are two types of capital gains: short-term, when you held the stock for less than twelve months and sold it at a gain, and long-term, when you held the stock for more than twelve months before selling at a gain. The difference is the way you are taxed. Short-term gains are taxed as ordinary income. Long-term gains are taxed at a maximum rate of 15 percent (through the year 2008).

"Capital loss carryover"

Let's turn the situation around and say that you purchased 100 shares of General Motors for $50 a share, a total investment of $5000. Let's say six years later the price of the shares fell to $2 and are now valued at $200. Your total loss would be $4800. If you have a capital loss greater than $3,000 for the year—that is, if your capital losses exceed your gains by more than $3,000—you won't be able to deduct all your losses this year.

However, you will be able to carry over any losses that exceed $3,000—in this case $1,800—and deduct them in future years. The losses will retain their status as short-term or long-term when you carry them over.

"I'm going to move my assets from one fund to another"

Mutual funds allow for flexibility and liquidity because investment companies allow you to exchange or sell your shares over the phone or online. For example, if you are in an aggressive growth fund and are uncomfortable with the volatility of the stock market, you can decide to exchange your funds for a growth-and-income fund, which has moderate risk. If your mutual fund is not held in a tax-deferred account like an individual retirement account, you are initiating a taxable event in the form of a capital gain or loss, so you want to consider the tax consequences.

DISCUSSIONS ON BUYING AND SELLING STOCKS

"She placed a trade for me"

Placing a trade means ordering a particular stock. The order states how many shares you want to buy and at what price. If you were working with a broker, here's how it would work:

1. You order 100 shares of Verizon through your broker.
2. Your stockbroker calls the order in to the trading desk.
3. The trading desk notifies the broker on the floor of the exchange.
4. The broker on the floor buys the shares and notifies the desk what it cost.
5. The desk calls your broker.
6. Your broker calls you to report the price and to confirm that the order was placed.

"I'm placing a market order"

This is the most common trade execution. If an investor put a market order on, say, Nordstrom (JWN), this means she is willing to pay the current market price, no matter the cost. It also means that your stock will be sold at the price at the time the order is placed.

"I'm placing a limit order"

A limit order reflects the price you are willing to pay for a stock. If you place a limit order to purchase 100 shares of American Express

(AXP) at $20 and the price of the shares fall to that specific price, the order will be executed either at that price or lower.

"I'm placing a good till cancelled (GTC) order"

As its name suggests, the order is not cancelled until you decide to do so. For example, if you call your broker (or enter the order online) and place an order to sell 1,000 shares of Company A as a limit order of $30 (the price you're willing to pay), if that order is not filled during the day it will automatically be cancelled at the close of business. But if the order is entered GTC then it will keep working until the shares are either sold at $30 or the order is cancelled. GTC orders are best used to buy or sell stock at price levels that are far away from the present price. So if Company A is currently trading at $30 and you want to buy 1,000 shares at $25 if and when it declined to that price, a GTC order would be helpful.

The expiration for GTC and limit orders is sixty to ninety days.

STOCK ANALYSIS AND RESEARCH

"The earnings report is good [bad, questionable, or inconclusive]"

An earnings report, also known as the earnings per share report, is the amount of earnings, or profits, of a company, divided by the number of shares of stock that are outstanding. Those who analyze stock use the earnings report to assess how well a company is performing.

"Its P/E is 19"

When someone talks about P/E, she means the price-to-earnings ratio. The P/E ratio is the price of a stock divided by its earnings per share. The higher the ratio, the greater the investment risk, because the current stock price represents the company's future potential earnings. The ratio is used to give an investor an idea of how much she is paying for the "earnings" of the stock. The question an investor asks is, "Can the company meet or exceed these expectations?" If the company's earnings don't grow, then the price of the stock will decrease to reflect the actual performance. The P/E is also called "times earnings" or sometimes "the multiple."

"I saw it in the Value Line"

Investors look to the Value Line Investment Survey as the Bible of stock research. You can find virtually anything about a company, if it is followed. The survey includes historical data, performance data, management team information, and a rating by analysts of whether the stock is a strong buy or one that should be held or sold.

"Morningstar ranked it five stars"

The Morningstar Mutual Fund Report is the Bible of mutual fund investing. It is a two-page research report that ranks mutual fund performance by a one- to five-star rating. The rankings are conducted every quarter. Because you are, or will become, an investor in mutual funds, I suggest that you review the report and visit the Morningstar website at www.morningstar.com. The Morningstar mutual fund rankings are readily accessible at your local library. One of my former clients says that the Morningstar guides gave her a good sense of how the funds offered by her employers had performed. By reading it, she got details on portfolio managers through their resumes, which increased her confidence in them. She said she sat immersed in reading graphs that illustrated how much $10,000 invested would have grown in ten years. The numbers and concepts were no longer abstract to her. This was actual performance.

"AAR predicts good things for that company"

The average annual return (AAR) is a measure of how an investment has performed over periods of time. Performance is measured over a month, a quarter, a year, and increments of three, five, and ten years. This gives an investor a sense of what the average performance has been on an annualized basis.

"It'll probably be a hostile takeover"

A hostile takeover occurs when another company or individual purchases a controlling interest against the will of a company's board of directors and shareholders. A stock confers a share of ownership in the company that issues it. If a company issued 1,000 shares, and you own 100 of them, you own a tenth of that company. If you own more than 500 shares, you own a majority or controlling interest in that company. When the company makes major decisions, the shareholders are given a proxy and must vote on them. The more shares you have, the more votes you get. If you own more than half of the shares, you always have a majority of the votes. In many respects, you can control the company.

BUYING BONDS WITH AN ADVISOR

You can ask a financial advisor what types of bonds are available and what she would recommend. The advantage to purchasing bonds through an advisor is that she can conduct research on your behalf; her firm may also have an inventory of bonds for sale. Another advantage is that the brokerage firm could be involved in bringing a new issue of bonds to the market, and one of the privileges of being a customer is having access to new issues. She can also buy bonds that trade on the secondary market—where you buy and sell bonds that were already issued and that were sold previously to investors and institutions that now want to sell their bonds. Both corporate and municipal bonds trade on the secondary market, or over-the-counter (OTC), which is an electronic exchange. Similar to the way buying and selling works on eBay, buyers who want to purchase bonds are matched with sellers who want to sell their bonds over-the-counter electronically. In this case, your broker places the orders on your behalf. If you don't feel confident researching bonds on your own, it makes sense to pay for the assistance of a financial advisor.

BUYING BONDS ON YOUR OWN

You can also do the research yourself and purchase bonds through an online discount broker such as www.fidelity.com or www.schwab.com. Discount and online brokers have access to bonds that trade on the secondary market and that trade on the OTC exchange. If you buy the bonds from a full-service broker, they normally include a markup.

Go to the Securities Industry and Financial Markets Association (SIFMA) website, www.sifma.org, and check out yields and other features of the various bonds.

BEFORE YOU BUY, RESEARCH

Decide What Type of Bond to Purchase

You'll want to select a bond that aligns with the goals and objectives of your investments. For example, if you will need the funds to pay for college tuition five years from now, choose a bond with that maturity date. A short-term bond matures in three years or less; an intermediate bond in five to ten years; and a long-term bond in ten years or more.

Find Out How the Bond is Rated

Pay close attention to a bond's rating to determine the issuer's ability to pay interest and return your principal. A high rating of AAA or Aaa (see chart in Chapter Five) generally means a secure bond. However, the trade-off is that the higher the rating, the lower the interest rate. Treasury bonds are considered the safest, which is why they generally pay lower interest rates than other bonds. You may find a corporate bond with a lower rating and fairly good rate of return. The hard part is assessing how stable a company will be over the life of the bond so you can get your money back.

Check to See if Your Bond Can Be Redeemed Early

A call feature allows the bond's issuer, whether a company, municipality, or government agency, the option to retire bonds early if it is in their interest to do so. When interest rates go down, a bond issuer has the option of paying it off before the maturity date so that it can issue new bonds at a lower rate. You, as the investor, have your cash back, but you're faced with a lower rate of return if you reinvest the money.

ONCE THE RESEARCH IS COMPLETED, PLACE AN ORDER

Step 1. Open a Brokerage Account

When you open an account you will need to transfer money into the account from your bank account.

Step 2. Indicate Which Bonds You Want to Buy and How Much You Want to Invest

Bonds are purchased in increments of a thousand and are priced in hundreds. For example, the following description was listed in the Fidelity Investment Online Inventory:

GE CAPITAL INTERNOTES

5.00000% 05/15/2016 at a price of 93.60.

These are GE Capital Notes that are paying an annual interest of 5% or $50 per bond annually.

Although the bond is priced at 93.60 the actual cost per bond is 933.60 per bond; because they are trading at a discount the actual yield or return is 5.35%.

Remember the formula: Amount/price = yield.

50.00/933.60 = (refer to yield chart on page 106). Keep in mind that the broker's commission is usually built into the bond price. Their actual cost may have been $910 and you paid $936; the difference or spread is what they make on selling you the bonds.

Step 3. Place the Trade

Indicate the number of bonds. Enter the CUSIP number, which is a numeric identification that corresponds to the bond description. This ensures that you purchase the specific bonds that you chose.

Step 4. Await Verification

The brokerage firm will verify that you have enough money in your account to cover the transaction, and then it will buy the bonds.

Step 5. Get Confirmation of the Purchase

You should receive a trade notification after the trade has been confirmed within a few minutes of the transaction. The settlement date is three business days later and when funds must be available for payment.

Step 6. The Bonds Will Now Be Listed in Your Brokerage Account

Their value will be reflected on your monthly or quarterly statement. The bonds will be held in your account for safekeeping and the interest will be credited every six months.

BUYING GOVERNMENT BONDS DIRECT

You can buy Treasury bonds directly from the federal government at regularly scheduled auctions through your brokerage account. You can also purchase them at www.treasurydirect.gov by opening an account that allows you to purchase Treasury bills, notes, or bonds directly from the Treasury. Establishing an online account is as easy as 1-2-3-4.

Step 1. Provide Your Personal Information

To open an account online you'll need to provide the following information: Social Security number or Taxpayer Identification Number; driver's license number or state ID and expiration date; bank routing number and account number of the checking or savings account you'd like to use to set up your TreasuryDirect account; e-mail address. You'll need an Internet browser that supports 128-bit encryption. (You will be prompted to download an updated web browser if you have an older version.)

Step 2. Await verification

You should receive verification of the information you provided in an e-mail within ten minutes.

Step 3. Choose a Password, Password Reminder, and Additional Security Questions

An e-mail with your account number will be sent to you. You will also receive an Access Card in the mail within the next two weeks. Your account number, password, and Access Card are needed to log in to your TreasuryDirect account.

Step 4. Decide What Type of Bonds to Purchase

You'll want to select a bond that aligns with the goals and objectives of your investment.

Treasury bills mature in less than one year and are sold at a discount from their face value.

Treasury notes have maturities of two, three, five, seven, and ten years and pay interest every six months.

Treasury bonds pay interest every six months and mature in thirty years.

Treasury Inflation-Protected Securities (TIPS) are adjusted by changes in the Consumer Price Index, pay interest every six months, and are issued with maturities of five, ten, and twenty years.

Savings Bonds are a low-risk savings product that earns interest while protecting you from inflation. EE/E Savings Bonds pay interest based on current market rates for up to thirty years. Electronic EE Savings Bonds are sold at face value at TreasuryDirect.

Placing an Order Online in TreasuryDirect

1. Enter your account number and access password.
2. Select who the security is being purchased for, as indicated by the name or names on the account.
3. Select the type of security: Treasury bill, note, TIPS, or savings bond.
4. Schedule the date that you want to purchase the security. A calendar will appear to show you the dates of auctions and availability of the security.
5. Verify the type of security and place the order.
6. Funds will be transferred from the account that was verified when you opened your TreasuryDirect account and your transaction is verified via e-mail.

BOND TIPS

- Shop and compare before you purchase. Obtain at least two quotes on your bonds from different companies in order to determine the markup or commission. Unlike stocks, bond inventories vary day-to-day and if you are buying smaller amounts, the commission could be more than the return.

- Diversify. It is better to own several different types of bonds with different yields. If you do not have funds available to diversify, you should consider investing in bonds funds.
- Issuers are developing all types of bonds to meet specific needs. For example, Treasury Inflation-Protected Security (TIPS) bonds were created specifically to address the investors' inflation concerns. Be on the lookout for the introduction of new products.
- If you do not need current income, you should buy zero-coupon bonds. They are purchased at a discount to their face value, and the interest is the difference in the maturity value, similar to savings bonds. For example, you would purchase the bond for $500 today and in ten years you would receive $1,000. The difference of $500 is the interest that was not paid to you over the period.

....

Bonds can provide you with the balance and diversification that allows you to fill your purse during any economic cycle.

One of the most effective ways to build wealth is to set up fail-safe ways of paying your purse first. You can accomplish this through automatic investment programs in both mutual funds and stocks. Systematic investment programs help you acquire discipline, focus, and the savings habits needed to stay the course through the ups and downs of the economy.

Savings bond payroll savings plans: Allow you to purchase savings bonds through payroll deduction. Visit www.treasurydirect.gov to set up an account through payroll deduction as described in Chapter Five.

Mutual fund debit programs: These are also known as automatic account builder programs. You will authorize mutual fund companies to debit a preset amount from a bank savings or checking account to buy fund shares on a weekly, monthly, or quarterly basis. Many mutual fund companies reduce their minimum investment to establish accounts from $2,500 to $50 monthly. These types of plans are great for long-term goals like retirement planning and college savings. If a mutual fund offers this program, that information will usually be listed under the payment methods. You will need to provide your bank information and a copy of a voided check or a deposit slip.

Mutual fund reinvestment programs: Reinvesting all dividends and capital gains distributions into more shares of the fund provides an additional method for helping your investments grow. When you establish an account with a mutual fund, simply check the box on your initial application indicating that you would like to reinvest your dividends and capital gains.

Direct stock purchase programs: A number of companies allow you to purchase their stock direct, without using a broker. To determine if a public company will allow you to directly invest, visit the investor relations area of their website. Many Fortune 500 companies such as Walmart, Disney, and Procter & Gamble have this program. Visit www.computershare.com for access to hundreds of companies with this type of program.

Dividend reinvestment plans (DRIPs): Companies offer their shareholders the opportunity to reinvest their dividends in more shares of the company, and in some cases, buy additional shares at a discount with little or no brokerage commissions. You must already own company shares in order to enroll in a dividend reinvestment plan. This is an excellent way to automatically accumulate additional shares of a company.

Small investor stock purchase programs: websites such as www .buyandhold.com and www.sharebuilder.com allow investors to conduct research and establish automatic investment programs and purchase stocks for as little as $4. Unlike investing through a broker with account minimums of a $1,000 or more plus commissions, these online accounts allow you to purchase fractional shares monthly for a nominal transaction fee. These are a great starter investment accounts that can show our daughters how to research and invest in stocks. Your daughter can also build a fantasy stock portfolio and "invest" at www.401kidz.com, which is sponsored by Sharebuilder.

Periodic investment programs: These plans are contractual agreements that require you to invest for longer periods of time, typically ten to fifteen years. The commissions assessed on these types of programs can be up to 50 percent of your monthly investments in the first five years. Always check the prospectus to see the amount of commission being charged. These plans place a premium on convenience but can be hazardous to the wealth of your purse. Visit www.finra.org to read their investor alerts.

ORGANIZING YOUR PURSE

In order to keep track and monitor your investment programs, it is important to have a system that allows you to take a snapshot of your portfolio and net worth. Here are a few ideas that can assist you in keeping your purse in order.

SOFTWARE PROGRAMS

Quicken Personal Finance software: This software program allows you to consolidate the information from all of your accounts in one place. You can have your bank and investment accounts automatically downloaded to this program and bring record keeping into the twenty-first century.

Microsoft Money: This software program allows you to consolidate banking and investment accounts. You can also download account information from other investment and mutual fund companies.

PNC Virtual Wallet: PNC Bank has online banking software that allows you to manage your finances virtually from anywhere. This online banking software focuses on managing cash flow and savings goals.

Online banking platforms: Most of the major banks have online banking sites which allow you to pay bills online and consolidate your outside investment accounts. Bank of America, Wells Fargo, and PNC Bank all have this type of service to help you monitor your cash flow and track your net worth.

WEB-BASED FINANCIAL TOOLS

Mvelopes.com (www.mvelopes.com) is an online expense management system that was based on a manual bill paying system used by many families. This is a great tool for budgeting and cash flow management.

Foonance (www.foonance.com) is a personal finance service designed with families, couples, and the average person in mind. Foonance lets users quickly import their bank statements and other financial information so that new users can get started managing their money quickly. Users can set up different transfers between accounts and schedule transactions such as mortgage and student loan payments.

Wesabe (www.wesabe.com) is an interactive Web-based personal finance monitoring tool. This tool lets you manage your finances by directly interacting with your bank account, savings account, or credit card, putting it a step above other financial tools that only reflect the information you remember to input.

Money2Manage (www.money2manage.com) allows you to manage multiple accounts so that you can keep track of several different transactions in one place. It is also easy to set up a list of payees so that you can keep track of who needs to be paid what and when they need to be paid. You can easily create categories to make it easier to track different types of accounts.

Spendji (www.spendji.com) is an all-in-one personal finance management tool for families and friends who have a great deal of planning to do. The site helps families create budgets that the entire family can follow; this includes handling bills, groceries, discretionary spending, and much more. Families and friends can also use Spendji to communicate and share important dates and news.

Microsoft Money and Quicken provide you with the most comprehensive method of tracking and recording your financial information, and they make filing taxes a breeze. However, the initial setup will require you to obtain all of your account records and passwords, which can take more than a few hours of your time. The Web-based programs focus on budgeting and cash flow management and most have communities that offer money tips and support. If you are intimidated by all of the bells and whistles, start with your existing banking relationship.

Adding to your purse and monitoring your progress is how you assess if you are on track to achieve your goals. Remember, it's not how much money you put in your purse; it's how much you keep and grow that increases your net worth.

Paying our purses forward is how we ensure that all young women adopt Wealthy Habits. Every girl should have a purse of her own, and that requires guidance from role models who can pave the way. Here are a few purse basics that are designed to make sure her pumps are on the right foot.

ACCOUNTS IN HER NAME

Bank and investment accounts can be established in your daughter's name. These accounts are called either Uniform Gift to Minors (UGMA) or Uniform Transfer to Minors (UTMA), depending upon the state where the child resides. A parent or another adult must be named as trustee.

They have some definite advantages and disadvantages:

- For children under the age of fourteen, currently the first $850 of yearly income from dividends or interest earned in the account is tax-free. If you are saving several thousand dollars in the child's name, you may want to consider other tax-advantaged accounts such as 529's. The funds must be used for the child but the trustee can decide how the funds can be spent.

- One disadvantage is that when your daughter reaches the age of maturity (age eighteen to twenty-one, depending on the state) the child then owns the account and may spend the assets as she wants. But we are laying a financial foundation and based on the ground rules we've shared with our daughters, spending money wisely should not present a problem.

ESTABLISHING CREDIT IN HER NAME

Start establishing credit for your daughter in her teens. Explain the pitfalls of overspending on a credit card to her and how credit scores impact your ability and cost to borrow.

There are five factors that establish a credit score.

- Have all the payments been paid on time?
- How much debt is outstanding in her name?
- How long has that credit line been in existence?
- How many new credit lines have been established?
- Having experience with various types of credit, such as installment loans and revolving credit cards.

By establishing credit early, your child will have a jump start on establishing her credit history. This will make it easier to purchase an automobile or home with a better interest rate.

There are two ways to establish credit for your teen:

Authorized user: Simply call the bank card company and tell them that you would like to add a name to your bank card as an authorized user. You will need to supply the Social Security number of the new authorized user to the bank card company. You do not have to give the child the bank card; they are simply an "authorized user." In about thirty days your child will have an established credit history.

Secured credit card: A secured card requires a cash collateral deposit that becomes the credit line for that account. For example, if you put $500 in the account, you can charge up to $500. The reason for having a secured card goes far beyond being able to buy stuff online. It's a start for building a good credit history. Verify that the issuing secured card company reports to all three of the credit reporting bureaus. It may take three to six months or more to establish a credit history. The longer the secured account is in existence and in good standing, the better the credit score will be.

It won't be long before they are headed to college where credit cards will be readily available. Learning how to use credit responsibly is one of the most important skills we can pass on to our daughters. What they don't know about credit will cost them dearly.

PAYING FOR COLLEGE

A college education can play a tremendous role in your daughter's ability to create a full purse. Women with college degrees earn 70 percent more than those without, according to research conducted in 2005 by the College Board. The good news is that there are many ways to pay for college, and they don't all involve emptying your purse or sacrificing other financial goals. With knowledge, planning, and saving, a college education for our daughters is within reach.

529/COLLEGE SAVINGS PLAN

These plans are a specialized account earmarked for college use only. (The number 529 is the Internal Revenue Code designation for this type of account.) Earnings in 529 accounts grow tax-free while you save money. As the parent or grandparent, you control the account. You can invest your contributions in different types of mutual funds with varying degrees of risk. One big advantage to a 529 account is that there are no income limitations. This simply means that no matter how much money you earn each year, you can open this type of account—aunts and grandmothers can establish these plans as well. Money invested in 529's can be used to pay for tuition to any college in the United States, which gives the student a lot of flexibility.

529 PREPAID TUITION ACCOUNT

When it comes to college savings, I give this my highest vote hands down. These plans are usually state-specific and their features can vary as a result. This type of account does exactly what its name implies: it prepays future tuition cost. Anyone can contribute to this account and make either a one-time lump sum payment or pay in monthly installments. The advantage of this account is that the cost of tuition and fees are frozen at the time you sign up. This means that the state has calculated the amount that must be paid for tuition and fees in the future; regardless of how much college costs increase, you won't pay any more than you expected to when you signed up for the program. Visit www.collegesavings.org to obtain information on programs that are offered throughout the United States. Prepaid tuition programs are a great way to ensure that your child has the money needed when she is ready to attend college. This plan only covers the cost of tuition. You must have additional savings to pay for room and board.

COVERDELL EDUCATION IRA (CESA)

An education IRA is an investment account that is established specifically for college savings. Two thousand dollars per year can be deposited into this account for children under the age of eighteen. Contributions are not tax-deductible, so there is no immediate saving on income taxes. But the good news is that the money and assets in this type of account grow tax-free. Even better, there are no taxes due when the money is withdrawn to pay for college. Money in an education IRA can be used to cover tuition, books, and room and board.

A PURSE OF HER OWN

Time sure flies—now she has graduated from college and is a lot better prepared than you or I were at her age. We've come full circle, and it is imperative that you encourage her to contribute to the employer-sponsored retirement program instead of splurging on the brand new 200SX sports car. A few dollars into a Roth IRA that she can have access to in five years to buy her first home is also an option. But of course, that was her plan anyway because she received her copy of *Purse* on her fourteenth birthday. The pages are worn and some of the passages are highlighted and she's wondering which mutual fund to invest in if her goal is to buy a home in five years. Yep. That's our Purse Girl. Pass the purse forward, ladies.

NOTES

Using Your Purse for Protection

xi. *on a rain-soaked road near Dallas:* "A Guy Witnesses an Accident When Still on the Phone," youtube.com/watch?v=mL1Gbbeheek.

xiii. *The purse has long been a reflection of our economic power:* Stephanie Pedersen, *Handbags: What Every Woman Should Know* (Devon, England: David & Charles, 2006).

xv. *has said that she was:* Laura Roberts, "K Rowling: I Considered Suicide As a Struggling Single Mother," *The Daily Mail Online*, March 2008. www.dailymail.co.uk/news/article-542608/JK-Rowling-I-con sidered-suicide-struggling-single-mother.html#.

xvi. *Mary Kay Ash, founder of Mary Kay Cosmetics:* Kathleen Hall, "Intuition," *Pink,* June 2008, 24.

xvi. *Dartmouth University Tuck School of Business Professor:* Lindsay Holloway, "Come Together," *Entrepreneur,* June 2008, 35.

xxiv. *Studies tracking men and women:* "Wall Street's Gender Agenda," Saskia Scholtes, *The Financial Times,* Business Life, February 28, 2007, 11.

One: Getting to the Bottom of Your Purse Before You Invest

2. *six million stay-at-home moms:* Lisa Belkin, "Why Dad's Resumé Lists 'Carpool'," *The New York Times,* June 12, 2008, G1.

6. *According to Dr. Joan C. Williams, director:* Joan C. Williams, "Opt-Out Revolution Revisited," *The American Prospect,* February 19, 2007. www.prospect.org/cs/articles?articleId=12495.

13. *a Prudential Financial study released in 2008:* Michelle Singletary, "Despite Strides, Women Still Tripped Up by Confidence Gap," *The Washington Post,* August 24, 2008, F01.

16. *Karen Finerman, 44, is one of the most:* Marianne MacDonald, "She's Worth $100m, Runs a $400m Hedge Fund, Has Two Sets of Twins and Four Nannies," *The Observer,* September 9, 2007. www.guardian .co.uk/lifeandstyle/2007/sep/09/features.woman5.

21. *In 2007, India grew 86 percent in dollar terms:* William Power, "How Well Do You Know . . . Global Investing?" *The Wall Street Journal,* May 5, 2008, R7.

21. *That same year, China's growth surged 59 percent:* Jim Yardley, "China's Leaders Try to Impress and Reassure World," *The New York Times,* August 9, 2008, 1.

21. *577 million mobile phone accounts:* "Retail and Shopper Trends: Asia Pacific 2008," The Nielsen Company. www.au.nielsen.com/site/ documents/ShopperTrends08_AP_report.pdf.

23. *But that autoworker wouldn't be considered unusual:* Martin Fackler, "Japanese Wives Sweat in Secret as Markets Reel," *The New York Times,* September 16, 2007.

Two: Falling in Love with Stocks at First Sight

33. *The FDIC was created in 1933:* Daniel Gross, "A Chicken Little Tale for Adults," *Newsweek,* July 28, 2008, 19.

39. *MBA students at the prestigious Wharton School of Business:* Marci Alboher, "Hot Ticket in B-School: Bringing Life Values to Corporate Ethics," *The New York Times,* May 29, 2008, C5.

51. SmartMoney's *Janet Paskin writes:* Janet Paskin, "Advice on Advisors," *SmartMoney,* May 2008, 72.

53. *under the leadership of Anne Mulcahy:* Olga Kharif, "Anne Mulcahy Has Xerox by the Horns," *BusinessWeek,* May, 29, 2003. www.busi nessweek.com/technology/content/may2003/tc20030529_1642_tc111 .htm.

54. *who was succeeded in 2009 by Ursula Burns:* Heidi Evans, "Ursula Burns to Head Xerox, Will Be First Black Woman to be CEO of Fortune 500 Company," *Daily News,* May 23, 2009. www.nydailynews .com/money/2009/05/23/2009-05-23_1st_black_woman_xerox_ceo .html#ixzz0HV50twLr&B.

54. *led by Indra Nooyi:* Michael Useem, "America's Best Leaders: Indra Nooyi, PepsiCo CEO," *US News & World Report,* November 19, 2008. www.usnews.com/articles/news/best-leaders/2008/11/19/americas -best-leaders-indra-nooyi-pepsico-ceo.html.

Three: Using What You Know About Diets to Invest

57. *In the spring of 2008, a nutritional study:* Will Dunham, "Research Debunks Health Value of Guzzling Water," Reuters, April 2, 2008. www .reuters.com/article/healthNews/idUSN0236679720080402.

57. *The late diet expert Dr. Robert Atkins:* Robert C. Atkins, *Atkins for Life: The Complete Controlled Carb Program for Permanent Weight Loss and Good Health* (New York: St. Martin's Press, 2003), 103.

59. *puts his money where his mouth is:* Dyan Machan, "The World's Greatest Investors," *SmartMoney,* August 2008, 48.

60. *As Dharma spiritual leader Ken Wilber has pointed out:* Andrew Cohen and Ken Wilber, "What It Means to Be a Man," *Enlightenment,* August–October 2008, 44.

61. *In the early 1980s, the U.S. personal savings:* Peter S. Goodman, "Economy Fitful, Americans Start to Pay as They Go," *The New York Times,* February 5, 2008, A1.

63 *In a study published in the July 2008:* Katherine Hobson, "4 Ways a Food Diary Can Help You Lose Weight," *U.S. News & World Report,* July 12, 2008. www.health.usnews.com/articles/health/living-well-usn/ 2008/07/08/4-ways-a-food-diary-can-help-you-lose-weight.

65. *Pleasant Rowland, who sold her American Girl doll:* "All the News in the

World of Dolls!" Dolls This Week Archives, May 5, 2000. collectdolls
.about.com/library/blast53.htm.

66. *Born in 1867, this daughter of former slaves:* A'Lelia Bundles, *On Her
Own Ground: The Life and Times of Madam C.J. Walker* (New York:
Scribner, 2002).

66. *a ravenous appetite for wealth:* Frank Lalli, "How She Turned $5,000 into
$22 Million (and How Your Might Too . . .)," *Money,* January 1, 1996.
www.money.cnn.com/magazines/moneymag/moneymag_archive/
1996/01/01/207651/index.htm.

69. *A 1980–2008 study of 5,000:* Tara Parker-Pope, "Instead of Eating to
Diet, They're Eating to Enjoy," *The New York Times,* September 17,
2008, F1.

70. *responsible for more than 90 percent:* Katy Marquardt, "Putting Together the Pieces," *Kiplinger's Success with Your Money,* Winter 2007,
40–42.

72. *He told Money magazine:* Kesley Abbott, Max Alexander, Suzanne
Barlyn, et al., "The Smartest Advice I Ever Got," *Money,* August 2008.
www.money.cnn.com/galleries/2008/pf/0807/gallery.smartest_advice
.moneymag/17.html.

73. *Jean-Marie Eveillard, former manger:* Ibid. Suzanne Barlyn

73. *Although the famed Mayo Clinic has reported:* Michael Picco, M.D., "Do
Detox Diets Offer Any Health Benefits?" April 22, 2008. www.mayo
clinic.com/health/detox-diets/AN01334.

74. *when McDonald's began accepting credit:* Donna Rosato, "Life Without
Plastic," *Money,* July 2008, 92.

74. *people eat more when there's:* Jane Bennett Clark, "5 Ways to Whip
Inflation When You Shop at a Warehouse Club," *Kiplinger's Personal
Finance,* August 2008, 58.

Four: Knowing When to Hold Stocks and When to Fold 'Em

79. *the chief executive of Capital Institutional:* Christina Binkley, "General
Counsel: Fashion Fuels a Friendship," *The Wall Street Journal,* July 31,
2008, D8.

79. *on retainer for up to $10,000 a month:* Tony Dokoupil, "The $10,000-a -Month Psychic," *Newsweek,* June 30, 2008, 44–45.

80. *co-founding the iRobot Company:* Jessical Siegel, "Mother of Invention," *Pink,* September/October 2008, 52–56.

82. *When measuring overall price movement:* Paul J. Lim, "In a Downturn, Buy and Hold or Quit and Fold?" *The New York Times,* July 27, 2008, Business section, 5.

83. *As far back as 1998, University of California:* Brad M. Barber and Terrance Odean, eds., "Boys Will Be Boys: Gender, Overconfidence, and Common Stock Investment," *The Quarterly Journal of Economics,* February 2001, 262–292.

83. *A 2005 Digital Look survey also found:* "Women 'Better Investors than Men,'" BBC News, June 2005. www.news.bbc.co.uk/1/hi/business/4606631.stm.

84. *returns decrease as motion increases:* Whitney Tilson and John Heins, "Why We Own Berkshire," *Kiplinger's Personal Finance,* August 2008, 22.

84. *the more people check stock prices:* Jason Zweig, "Should You Fear the Ostrich Affect? *The Wall Street Journal,* September 13–14, 2008, B1.

84. *in a magnetic refrigerator frame:* Janice Revell, "How to Keep Your Cool in a Dangerous Market," *Money,* April 2008, 75.

89. *by answering the following questions:* Jason Zweig, "Should You Fear the Ostrich Effect?"

Five: The Closer I Get to My Goals, the Better Bonds Make Me Feel

101. *WHUR radio, which was:* Lynn Norment, "Ms. Radio," *Ebony,* May 2000. www.findarticles.com/p/articles/mi_m1077/is_7_55/ai_61963167/.

Six: A Pooling of Purses: Purchasing Mutual Funds

121. *had put $11 trillion into funds:* Katry Marquardt, "Putting Together the Pieces," *Kiplinger's Success with Your Money,* Winter 2007, 42.

136. *knows how to set up the most efficient of systems:* Sue Shellenbarger, "Triple Threat? Not for This Family," *The Wall Street Journal,* February 27, 2008. www.online.wsj.com/article/SB120412427444196805.html.

Seven: Feathering Your Purse for Retirement

143. *An estimated 51 percent:* Sam Roberts, "51% of Women Are Now Living Without Spouse," *The New York Times,* January 16, 2007. www .nytimes.com/2007/01/16/us/16census.html.

151. *employees have this kind of professional advice:* Tim Paradis, "401(k) Investors May See Returns Suffer," Yahoo! Finance, December 3, 2007. www .finance.yahoo.com/focus-retirement/article/103961/401k-Investors -May-See-Returns-Suffer?mod=retirement-401k.

151. *losing one percentage point of annual:* Walter Updegrave, "The Smart Way to Get Help With Your 401(k)," *Money,* August 2008, 47.

153. *cut your retirement savings by as much as 22 percent:* "More Americans Are Dipping into Their Retirement Funds," *The Wall Street Journal,* July 17, 2008, D5.

157. *a baby boomer earning a final salary of $75,000:* Emily Brandon, "Playing the Waiting Game," *Newsweek,* February 11, 2008, 50.

Eight: Passing On What You've Learned

164. *left her enough to pay her taxes:* Barbara Presley Noble, "A Few Thousand Women, Networking," *The New York Times,* March 27, 1994. www.query.nytimes.com/gst/fullpage.html?res=9F04E3D8113CF934 A15750C0A962958260.

164. *learn financial literacy:* Steven Goldberg, "Badly in Need of Financial Education," Kiplinger.com, May 12, 2008. www.kiplinger.com/col umns/value/archive/2008/va0513.htm.

164. *summer camp for inner city students:* "Money Matters For Youth," www .wxyz.com (Channel 7 Action News, Detroit), July 22, 2008. www .wxyz.com/content/news/dwym/story/Money-Matters-For-Youth/ jgrDlgXg0Uu_vDswdn7dkA.cspx.

164. *Arial Elementary Community Academy:* Noah Isackson, "Mellody Hobson," *Time,* December 17, 2004. www.time.com/time/magazine/ article/0.9171.1009758.00.html.

166. *with an interest in political science:* Bill Slocum, *Darien Magazine,* February 2006. www.mofflypub.com/Moffly-Publications/New-Canaan -Darien-Magazine/February-2006/Investing-Savvy/.

DEBORAH OWENS'S ACKNOWLEDGMENTS

I would like to thank the many people who made this book possible. First and foremost, my committed literary agent, Regina Brooks, the wearer of many hats. To our editor, Sulay Hernandez, who took the risk on a concept and molded our ideas into a book we can all be proud of. To Carlos Falchi, who understands that a woman's purse is an investment and style is for every woman. To Brenda Lane Richardson, whose creativity helped to create the book I envisioned. And finally, my husband, Terry Owens, who cheered us all on to the very end.

BRENDA LANE RICHARDSON'S
ACKNOWLEDGMENTS

I am always grateful to the Great Creator for continued inspiration and love. I am grateful also for Regina Brooks, agent extraordinaire, and Deborah Owens for her intelligence and unflagging good nature. My thanks also to Jim Kasson for reading our early manuscript, and our editor, Sulay Hernandez, who had the creative vision to imagine what *Purse* could become. I am thankful for the continued support of the Reverend Dr. William Mark Richardson; our children, H. P. Worthington III, Mark Richardson Jr., Carolyn Richardson; and our grandson, Tiger Kali Worthington. I am grateful beyond measure for support from the highly talented purse designer, Carlos Falchi, and his assistant and daughter, Kate Falchi. Finally, thank you to my professors at New York University's Silver School of Social Work.

INDEX